SEW A SAMPLER

SEW A SAMPLER

DOROTHEA KAY

Adam & Charles Black · London

First published 1979
A & C Black (Publishers) Limited
35 Bedford Row, London WC1R 4JH

ISBN 0 7136 1996 1

Printed in Great Britain by Sackville Press Billericay
Limited, England.

CONTENTS

LIST OF ILLUSTRATIONS

The Praise of the Needle

To all disperséd sorts of Arts and Trades
I write the needle's praise (that never fades).
So long as children shall be got or borne,
So long as garment shall be made or worne,
So long as Hemp or Flax, or Sheep shall bear
Their linnen-woolen fleeces yeare by yeare,
So long as silk-worms with exhausted spoyle,
Of their own entrails, for men's gain shall toyle,
Yea, till the world be quite dissolved and past,
So long at least, the needle's use shall last.

The Needle's Excellency
John Taylor

I
INTRODUCTION

"We Hermia ....
Have with our needles created both one flower
Both on one sampler, sitting on one cushion"

A Midsummer Night's Dream

So Shakespeare described the preoccupations of a normal girlhood and so the situation remained for centuries. Fathers and brothers might depart to serve the King, Cromwell, the Jacobites or to fight the Spanish, but the girls left behind quietly got on with their sewing. Strangely enough it is they who have lasting memorials, when the individual heroisms of their menfolk have merged into the general pattern of history, and they who by hours of work and patient industry have encapsulated an era of children's education for us to wonder at.

Everyone is familiar with the charm of samplers, their patterns and stitchery, the fineness of the work, and above all, the tender age of the executants. How is it possible, we exclaim, knowing our own ham-fisted efforts, that children should show such expertise? The answer of course is that our forefathers had a different time scale from ours and their priorities were different. In times when the efficient running of a household and the clothing of its members depended upon the skill of women, it is understandable that a needle was among the first tools put into the infant hand, and often before a pen. The pen is mightier than the sword, but many generations of mothers knew that the needle was more useful than either, and they saw to it that their children were well grounded in fine needlework while still at their knees.

Visitors to great houses will sometimes be amazed to see chair and settee covers, cushions and footstools worked by the lady and her children. These have survived because of their sheltered habitat, but they are not really an isolated phenomenon. It is simply that lower down the social scale the work was not so ambitious, and with the passage of time and hard usage was worn out and discarded. Anyone who understands the steady descent of linen from best use to everyday, to dust covers, to floor cloths, will understand why the household goods of former generations have perished. This process may have taken many years, but because the labour that went into their making was so considerable, the last possible bit of wear was extracted from them before they were finally discarded. In the production of these goods mothers recruited their daughters at an early age. Schools took over where mothers left off, and an important part of the curriculum was the teaching of the various branches of needlework.

Economic necessity was further re-inforced by moral ethic. Dickens' Little Dorrit seldom appears in her days of poverty without the needlework with which she supported herself. The Dolls' Dressmaker in *Our Mutual Friend* snips and pins and sews, with alarming expertise in one so young, to support her drunken father, Caroline Helstone in *Shirley* has to produce perfect darns in a stocking cut into holes for the sheer virtue of making perfect darns in a stocking cut in holes. The Puritan ethic saw value in work for its own sake, and it found popular expression in the saying that Satan finds work for idle hands. This idea, applied to many generations, produced a prodigious amount of work. But while the wear and tear of ordinary household usage has ensured the disappearance of the actual household goods, the samplers, the learning pieces of the needlewomen, have survived and show an amazing collection of patterns and stitches and a very high standard of skill.

That the social structure which produced this phenomenon has broken up will cause no one to lament. But the would-be needlewoman of today, when looking at these samplers, must feel sorrow for the loss of skills. It is not too harsh to say that a generation or two enjoying the benefits of modern education has produced a society where many women are illiterate with the needle. The whole ethos of education and the use of leisure has changed, and the slow and painstaking acquisition of skill in fine needlework has had no place in general education in the middle decades of this century.

However, the desire to create fine work is still with us. The general perversity of life ensures that since machines became available to do the necessary work mechanically, women have become dissatisfied and spend long hours acquiring in maturity skills which in former times were learnt in childhood.

This book attempts to provide material for such needlewomen. Some temerity is needed to produce yet another craft book, but this one will perhaps fill a need for those who wish to explore our historical heritage and re-use some of the designs and stitches beloved of our ancestors. The sampler has been, and always will be, the vehicle whereby the needlewoman learns her craft and no apology is needed for using it here. The designs given are all based on or derived from historical examples and are intended firstly to encourage the needlewoman to try her hand, and secondly to stimulate an interest in historical needlework in this particular field. Many museums have collections of samplers and some have a tremendous number in their reserve collections which are available on request to the student.

The material of samplers, whether linen or wool, was usually very fine and not only is it impossible to get today, but would prove too time-consuming to work as most of the stitches involve counting the number of threads to be taken up by the needle. Material of the same type is available on a coarser scale and is called evenweave. This technical term implies that the threads in the warp and weft are even in number. The threads themselves are tightly spun so that the material is not felted and the threads can be easily separated. This is important, because in the type of embroidery used, called embroidery by the counted thread, the embroidery thread goes between the threads of the fabric. A blunt-ended or tapestry needle is used which makes this easy to achieve.

Evenweave linen is available in craft shops and is classified by the number of threads to the inch, but once the embroiderer knows the type of fabric to look for she will find that some furnishing fabrics are suitable and also some dress or skirt weight woollen cloths, and of course the single thread canvas sold for canvas work. Twelve threads to an inch can be regarded as coarse, forty threads as very fine. Tapestry needles are available to suit the different weights of material and thread. These are most satisfactory as the blunt end will not pierce the tightly spun thread. For starting and finishing use a crewel needle, for the sharp point will enter the fabric and with care it is possible to hide completely all finishings. This is a refinement which greatly adds to the beauty of reversible stitches such as double running stitch, when it is possible to produce work with no wrong side.

There exists a reasonable variety of embroidery threads, not always easily obtainable however, and it is up to the individual to experiment with what she finds available. A twisted thread such as coton perlé for example is likely to give more satisfaction than stranded cottons. A list of suggestions, along with details of materials and needles, will be found at the back of the book.

II
THE SAMPLERS

In this book the samplers are arranged chronologically, not in order of difficulty. The later ones tend to be easier in fact, as they are worked almost exclusively in cross stitch.

Historically, samplers were usually worked on very fine linen and were closely packed with intricate stitches and patterns. The samplers here consist of selected patterns from these originals, considerably increased in scale and occasionally simplified. They attempt to give the modern embroiderer an insight into this particular type of embroidery, and into the historical progression which took place in sampler making during the centuries when they were popular. They also try to re-state, by increasing the scale of work and by using modern materials, the undying charm of these old patterns.

Detailed plans for each sampler are given, and also a considerable amount of other material, so that alternative designs can be worked. Each of these samplers is preceded by an historical chapter relevant to the sampler and accompanied by the necessary stitch directions.

The samplers are made in varying types of material and counts of thread. Do not assume that a coarse material will necessarily be easy to work with. A fabric with a strongly twisted thread is easier to work with than one with a softer, thicker thread. In the first case, the fabric threads resist the needle, which passes sweetly through the material, and an accurate stitch is made. In the second case, the needle is inclined to foul the softer fabric threads and the clarity of the stitch suffers in consequence.

Take account also that the eye soon acclimatises itself to the scale of the work. The beginner is advised to look for a good even-weave material with a count of about twenty threads to the inch. It is difficult to be more specific, because though many types of fabric are made, their availability is uncertain.

One widely available type of material is Binca, Bincarette and Aida. Here fine cotton threads are bulked together and woven as one unit, making fabrics with a low thread count and clearly visible holes in

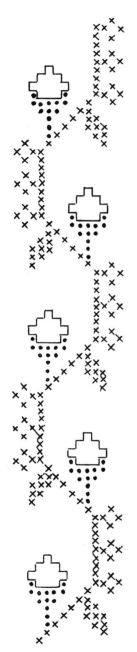

which to place the needle.

They are easy fabrics to work on, and excellent for use while mastering some stitches. They can be used successfully for embroidering strong patterns in stitches such as cross or rice stitch which are bold enough to stand out against the rather dominant weave of this type of material. Delicate patterns, like those of blackwork and double running do not look well on these fabrics however.

Scale

The scale of the work-charts is ten squares to the inch. Each square represents one cross stitch, or two threads of material. This makes ten cross stitches, over twenty threads, for each inch of chart. To calculate the size of the cross stitch designs worked on counts of material other than the actual one described, multiply the number of threads per inch in the chart by the length of the design, and divide by the number of threads per inch in the fabric which you intend to use.

Cross Stitch Example 1. For a fabric count of 30 threads per inch, and with a chart design measuring 6 in. long,

$$\frac{20 \times 6}{30} = 4,$$

so the worked design will be 4 in. long.

Cross Stitch Example 2. For a fabric count of 14, the chart design being $4\frac{1}{2}$ in. long,

$$\frac{20}{14} \times \frac{9}{2} = \frac{90}{14} = 6\frac{6}{14},$$

so the worked design will be approximately $6\frac{1}{2}$ in. long.

The same calculations must be made for the length and breadth of each design to find its exact size when worked.

For double running stitch patterns, a single square of chart represents one stitch, or three fabric threads. This makes ten stitches to the inch, over thirty fabric threads.

Double Running Stitch Example 3. For a fabric count of 20 threads per inch, the chart design being 8 in. long,

$$\frac{30 \times 8}{20} = 12,$$

so the worked design will be 12 in. long.

For satin stitch patterns a single square represents three stitches, one

A cross stitch border. The symbols represent contrasting colours

between each of three fabric threads. This makes thirty stitches to the inch, over thirty fabric threads.

Satin Stitch Example 4. For a fabric count of 26 threads per inch, the chart design being $3\frac{1}{2}$ in. long,

$$\frac{30}{26} \times \frac{7}{2} = \frac{105}{26} = 4\frac{1}{26},$$

so the worked design will be 4 in. long.

Rice stitch and Algerian eye stitch are worked over four threads. In these charts each small square represents two threads, making twenty threads to the inch of chart. This makes five complete rice stitches or five Algerian eye stitches.

Rice Stitch and Algerian Eye Stitch Example 5. For a fabric count of 16 per inch, the chart design being 6 in. long,

$$\frac{20 \times 6}{16} = \frac{15}{2} = 7\frac{1}{2},$$

so the worked design will be $7\frac{1}{2}$ in. long.

For oriental stitch and rococo stitch a single square of chart represents one thread, being ten threads to the inch.

Oriental Stitch and Rococo Stitch Example 6. For a fabric count of 30, the chart design measuring 4 in.,

$$\frac{10 \times 4}{30} \times \frac{4}{3} = 1\frac{1}{3},$$

so the worked design will be $1\frac{1}{3}$ in. long.

By using these simple calculations you will be able to use any of the designs in the book on material of any thread count and be certain of its eventual size when it is embroidered.

Drawn thread ground is prepared over four threads, one thread being drawn away and three left. In the chart each small square represents 2 threads, making 20 threads to the inch of chart.

Example 7 Drawn Thread Ground. For a fabric count of 30, the chart design being 6 in. long,

$$\frac{20 \times 6}{30} = 4,$$

so the worked design will be 4 in. long.

Border to work in double running stitch

Satin stitch border

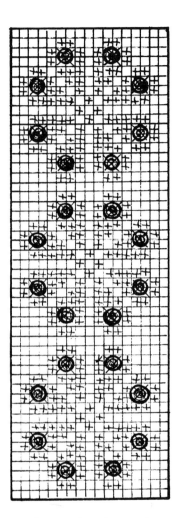

Drawn thread ground

Alternative cross stitch border

Colour

No serious attempt has been made to work the samplers in their original colours. These remain remarkably fresh and unfaded with the passage of time, but of course the type of silk is unobtainable. In the charts the different parts of each design have been clearly delineated, but it has been left to the individual worker to choose her own colours. This will give a great deal more pleasure to the worker and individuality to the work.

Method of work

There is plenty of evidence to show that samplers were usually worked on frames. The fineness of the fabric and the closeness of the stitches made this inevitable. Here the scale of the designs has been so much increased that to use a frame or not is a matter for personal preference.

There is something to be said on both sides. It is easier to see and count threads when the fabric is held in a frame. It is easier, in a frame, to sew certain stitches; for example in marking cross stitch, when the needle has to go into the centre of the stitch. Other stitches are much easier to work in the hand, especially those stitches where the needle does not often go down into the fabric. An example of this is detached buttonhole, which is very awkward to do when held stiffly in a frame.

A ring frame is a useful piece of equipment, in which the fabric is held firmly between two rings, one of which clips over the other. It is very easy to set up and easy to remove if desired.

After oversewing the edge of the material to prevent fraying, find the central vertical thread by carefully folding the material in two. Mark this thread with a tacking cotton along its entire length. If an all-round border is part of your design, find and mark the central horizontal thread also. These central lines of tacking should remain in position until the work is completed. They form the backbone of the design that will govern the placing of the main patterns, which are usually started from a central point. The tacking thread also is a guide to the placing of any side patterns, whose positioning relative to the central thread may need to be carefully counted.

Only when all the patterns have been worked should these guiding lines be removed. The edges of the sampler should then be finished in the style appropriate to its type. (See Chapter VII.)

Where diagrams are marked with an arrow, this indicates the point at which to start work.

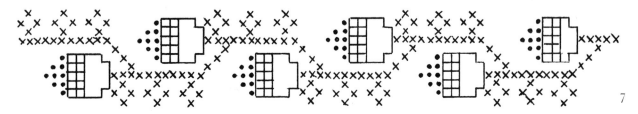

III
EARLY HISTORY

The familiar word 'sampler' has a long and respectable ancestry. Like so much of our vocabulary, it is a well travelled word and on its journey picked up several shades of meaning. Originally the Latin 'exemplum' meaning a copy, a pattern or a model, it came to us in its French form, exemplaire, and is one of the many thousands of words we received from across the Channel in the Middle Ages. Widely current by the sixteenth century it was being spelt variously, saumpler, sampler, or exampler.

From early days it had a double meaning; firstly a collection of patterns for the needlewoman, and a reference library of stitches, and secondly a piece of canvas embroidered by a beginner as a specimen of her skill. In the first centuries in which samplers flourished as a form of needlework these two meanings co-existed, but gradually the first died away leaving the second meaning the master of the field.

The practice of dating and signing samplers, later to become so much an essential part of the work, was not common in Tudor times. The earliest extant sampler, dated 1598 and signed Jane Bostocke, and with an inscription about the birth of one Alice Lee, is quite exceptional in this respect. (It can be seen in the Victoria and Albert Museum, London.) The fact that this sampler only came to light in 1960 makes one hope that other early samplers will be discovered.

Early samplers can be seen in a number of Museum collections. Some may be of a date prior to 1598, but it is impossible to be certain. The type of patterns used, the selection of stitches, the lay-out of the work, and the size, shape and type of background fabric all provide valuable clues whereby an expert can give them an approximate date.

Such samplers are always worked on a linen ground with silk and may be further embellished with silver and silver gilt threads. They vary in size, but are all of similar proportions, being rarely longer than twenty four inches and usually about twelve inches in width. They are known as 'spot' or 'random' samplers because the motifs on them are arranged in an apparently haphazard way. The workmanship on these samplers is so expert that they are judged to be the work of adult

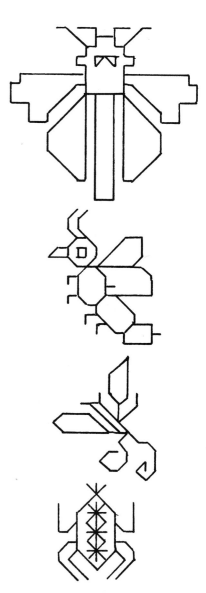

Small motifs for random placement

A charming small caterpillar motif

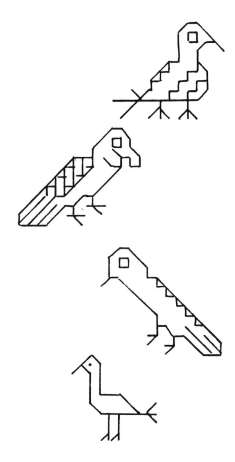

Little bird motifs for random placement

needlewomen.

Random samplers display an amazing range of pattern and stitch. There is a wide variety of geometric patterns and a good selection of flowers. Roses, carnations, tulips, pansies, vines, strawberries are intermingled with birds and animals. Here the domestic and the exotic are happily mixed. Dogs, stags, hares, swans, peacocks, lions and leopards proliferate and filling in the spaces between beasts and flowers are a multitude of flies, caterpillars, snakes, toads, fish and butterflies.

The stitches are equally varied. Tent, cross, rococo, double running, chain, back, buttonhole, two sided Italian cross, rice, long armed cross, Algerian eye, Roumanian, Florentine, Hungarian stitches – these are but a small selection of the stitches practised by the sixteenth century needlewoman.

If we were to rely only on the numerical evidence of these samplers, which have miraculously escaped the hazards which beset perishable goods, we should have a false idea about the popularity of sampler making in the sixteenth century. It was an activity sufficiently a part of the social scene to be commented upon by poets and dramatists. Skelton, writing in the first half of the century, was a poet who enjoyed the society of young ladies, and who observed their pursuits with interest. In his lament on the Death of Phyllyp Sparowe, he makes Jane, whose pet sparrow has been killed by a cat say

"I toke my sampler ones,
Of purpose, for the nones,
To sowe with stytchis of sylke
My sparow whyte as mylke."

Shakespeare, writing at the end of the century, has two allusions to sampler making. Literary references were fairly common by this time, and must reflect the fact that the work was a reasonably common activity.

This does not mean that every female child in the land was busy at her frame. Poets tend to reflect the life of high society, and Hermia and Helena (from *A Midsummer Night's Dream*) who sat upon a cushion busily sewing the same piece of linen (presumably one from each end) were of the nobility and members of the court circle.

The fine linen on which samplers were worked was itself a luxury item. This was stitched in silk thread and quite frequently embellished with silver thread and sequins, and even seed pearls. It is small wonder that samplers were cherished possessions not only for their practical value as works of reference.

In an age when items of clothing were passed from one generation to

Left. A very early sampler, probably seventeenth century, with a rich variety of flower, animal and bird motifs placed at random over the fabric.
By courtesy of the Victoria and Albert Museum.

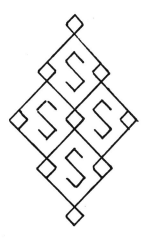

The 'S' pattern appears regularly in old samplers

another by will, it is natural to discover that samplers too were sometimes bequeathed. People are inclined to joke about Shakespeare leaving to his wife 'the second best bed', but many far humbler household goods were given a value which we, in our affluent throwaway society, find difficult to appreciate.

One of the earliest Elizabethan comedies, *Gammer Gurton's Needle*, throws some interesting light on this. The whole plot hinges on the fact that Gammer Gurton has lost her needle, and the house is thrown into turmoil as a result. She was a woman of considerable standing and substance, yet the fact that the house boasted only one sewing needle, and that it could not be easily replaced, is not regarded as extraordinary.

Early samplers then had an intrinsic value, being costly to make, but their real value lay in the fact that they were reference libraries of stitches and patterns for their owners. There is a charming description (quoted by Donald King in *Samplers*, H.M.S.O.) which tells how a rich man's wife would 'go to seke out her examplers, and peruse which work would doe best in a ruffe, whiche in a gorget, whiche in a sleeve . . . and to sitte her doune and take it forthe by little and little, and thus with her needle to passe the after noone with devising of thinges for her own wearynge'. This was written by Barnabe Riche in 1581.

Sampler patterns were no doubt often jealously guarded by their owners (as favourite recipes sometimes are to this day), and their number increased by the surreptitious copying of patterns belonging to friends and neighbours during social calls. Patterns were extremely hard to find in Tudor England, and the keen needlewoman had to make the most of any opportunity that offered itself.

At the beginning of this period pattern books of any kind were unknown, and patterns must have been passed from hand to hand, many of them filtering through from the continent, and even the Middle East. Some of the geometric patterns on early samplers are of very ancient origin and occur and recur in decorative work from the Egyptian period onwards. Especially notable are designs based on the X form, and designs of interlacing diamonds, where the central shapes are filled with the letter S. (See the pattern above.) Samplers were being made in the Middle East in the Middle Ages and Guildford Museum is the lucky possessor of some Coptic examples from North Africa.

During the Middle Ages England was far from being culturally isolated, with very strong French influences entering through the English Court. Any inter-marriage (and there were many) meant the introduction of a whole entourage of ladies, whose main occupation must have been needlework. The most famous examples of individuals influencing British needlework are Catherine of Aragon, a Spanish Princess and first wife of Henry VIII, and Mary Queen of Scots, educated in France to be the consort of Francis II of France, but doomed to spend the greater part of her life in captivity in either Scotland or England.

English society was also open to wider European influences through the network of the English wool and cloth trades. Both these commodities were sold in centres in the Low Countries and in Italy. These areas were justly famous for their craft work, particularly lace. Silk threads for embroidery must also have been imported from France and Italy.

During the sixteenth century there was a tremendous explosion of activity in travelling. Travellers such as Tradescant must have brought home not only rare plants, silks and spices, but also smaller domestic items designed to please their womenfolk. Fabrics, fancy braids, sewing silks and pattern books were an obvious choice of gifts for the home-bound traveller to include in his luggage.

The first pattern books were printed in Germany early in the sixteenth century. Others followed in France and Italy, and by the end of the century were in sufficient demand for English translations to be made. In 1591 a certain John Wolfe translated a French work under the title of *New and Singular Patterns and Works of Linen*. In 1596 William Barley published a book called *A booke of Curious and Strange Inventions, called the first part of Needleworkes*.

So began as a trickle what was to become a flood of pattern and craft books in later generations. Few of these early pattern books have survived because of the heinous but understandable practice of pricking the illustrations.

In the absence of any form of tracing paper the only way a pattern could be accurately reproduced was by this method. A piece of plain paper was placed behind the illustration and the outline was closely pricked with a needle, so that the shape was transferred onto the underneath sheet. Of course the zealous needlewoman pricked closely to get an accurate reproduction, but in so doing inevitably shortened the life of the book.

It is difficult to estimate the influence of pattern books on the making of early samplers because there are so many imponderables. Nobody knows the extent of the circulation, or the survival rate of the books. Some great libraries were already in existence, but the vast majority of homes must have had no, or few books. Books of theology would have pride of place, herbals and books of household management were also available, but rare indeed would be the household with a book of embroidery patterns on the shelf.

There is much we do not know about the making of early samplers, because their making was a private, domestic occupation, largely unchronicled and certainly not supported by needlework manuals of stitches. But the evidence which survives speaks to us of the amazing skill, vitality and invention of the needlewomen who made them.

Sampler 1. The Owl on the Vine

This is a small design taken from the sampler made by Jane Bostocke in 1598.

It is such a famous piece of work that it is worth describing in detail. Its size is $14 \times 16\frac{3}{4}$ in., and is worked on linen with silk, seed pearls and black beads. The motifs in the top section are widely spaced, and include the owl on the vine and a rose tree covered with hips on which sits a squirrel and a pelican in piety. This is an heraldic motif of a nest of fledglings being fed by the mother bird, who pecks her breast to give them sustenance. There are also two dogs, a bear, a hind, an heraldic leopard, a cowslip plant and a strip of daisy flowers. They are all in wonderful condition except for the little dog, Juno, whose silk has almost worn away, leaving just the needleholes behind.

Right. The earliest dated sampler, clearly marked 1598, worked on linen in silk, pearls and beads.
By courtesy of the Victoria and Albert Museum.

15

Below these, there is an alphabet, the signature sewn with seed pearls and the date, and the following inscription – ALICE : LEE : WAS : BORNE : THE : 23 : OF : NOVEMBER : BEING : TWESDAY : IN : THE : AFTER : NOONE : 1596.

The bottom two thirds of the sampler is tightly packed with all sorts of patterns, worked in back stitch, cross stitch, satin, chain, buttonhole and detached buttonhole stitch, to name just a few. Included among the patterns are some very fine examples of interlacing strapwork, a vine, and a strawberry pattern.

The Owl on the Vine given here is quite straightforward to work, using cross stitch, Method B. It is a little more difficult to work using marking cross stitch, Method D. (See page 21). Underneath it is a simple arrangement of different types of cross stitches.

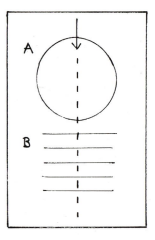

The layout for sampler 1

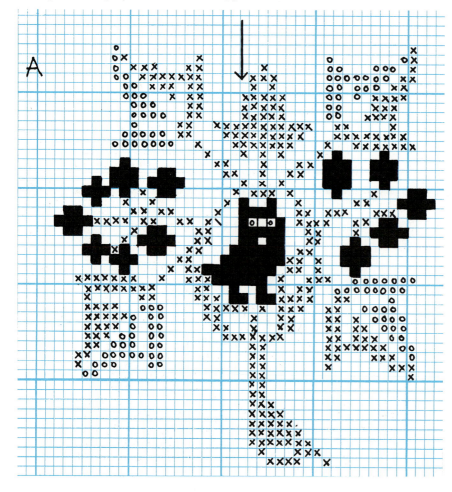

Left and above right. Patterns for sampler 1

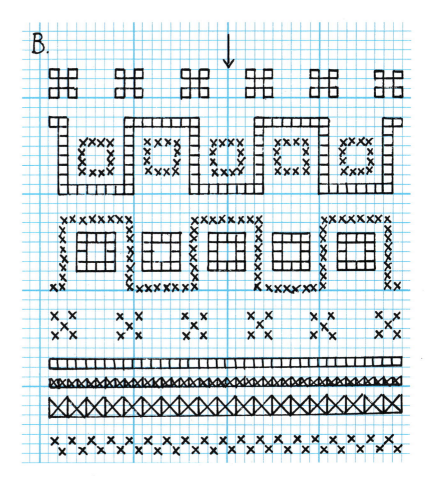

Count of linen: 28 threads to the inch.

Size of designs: A. $3 \times 2\frac{3}{4}$ in. – the vine

B. $2\frac{3}{4} \times 2\frac{3}{4}$ in. – the cross stitch exercise.

Thread used: Danish Flower Thread.

Overall size of material needed: (a) 10 in. × 7 in. (this allows for a hem-stitched edge) or (b) 12 in. × 8 in. (extra material allowed for mounting as a picture).

Size of finished work: $7\frac{3}{4} \times 4\frac{3}{4}$ in.

To adapt the design to other types of fabric, see Chapter II, under Scale, cross stitch.

To prepare the linen, see Chapter II under Method of Work.

Leave approximately $2\frac{3}{4}$ in. or $3\frac{3}{4}$ in. of linen at the top of the work, depending on the type of finishing you wish to have. Note that the centre of the design is marked on the chart. Begin your embroidery at the tip of the central vine leaf, making sure that your central tacking thread is correctly aligned to the centre line on the chart. If this leaf is correctly placed on the fabric, the rest of the design will work out satisfactorily. If you work methodically from the top leaf downwards, you will not find the counting of stitches and threads difficult.

Leave two threads between the design and the cross stitch patterns that are underneath it.

Leave four threads between each row that follows, except between rows five and six and six and seven, when two threads only are left.

Follow the chart for the placing of the rows.

1. Six small cross shapes worked in four-sided stitch (G). Work the two middle ones first. They are placed four threads to the right and left of the central tacking thread. If these are correctly placed the rest of the design will fall into its correct place.
2. A stepped line of four-sided stitch (G) enclosing squares of cross stitch (F).
3. The reverse of 2. A stepped line of cross stitch (F) enclosing squares of four-sided stitch (G).
4. The reverse of 1. Six square shapes in cross stitch (F).
5. A straight line of four-sided stitch (G).
6. A line of two sided Italian cross stitch, worked over two threads.
7. A line of two sided Italian cross stitch, worked over four threads.
8. Two rows of alternate cross stitch (E).

For finishing, see Chapter VII.

If you are an inexperienced needlewoman a very pretty sampler can be made without considering the back of the work. In which case do all the cross stitch parts of the work using Method B.

If however, you are experienced and enjoy a challenge, use the different types of reversible stitches given in the directions. With a little practice you will be able to produce a completely reversible piece of work. The twelve cross shapes are the most difficult to achieve. There is a singular pleasure to be had in doing this sort of work. If you can manage it, you will be approaching in skill the sixteenth century needlewomen who used these stitches.

The Hind and the Daisies is another set of patterns taken from the same source. It would make another sampler with the addition of some simple cross stitch patterns similar to those already given.

The hind and daisies motif from very early sampler

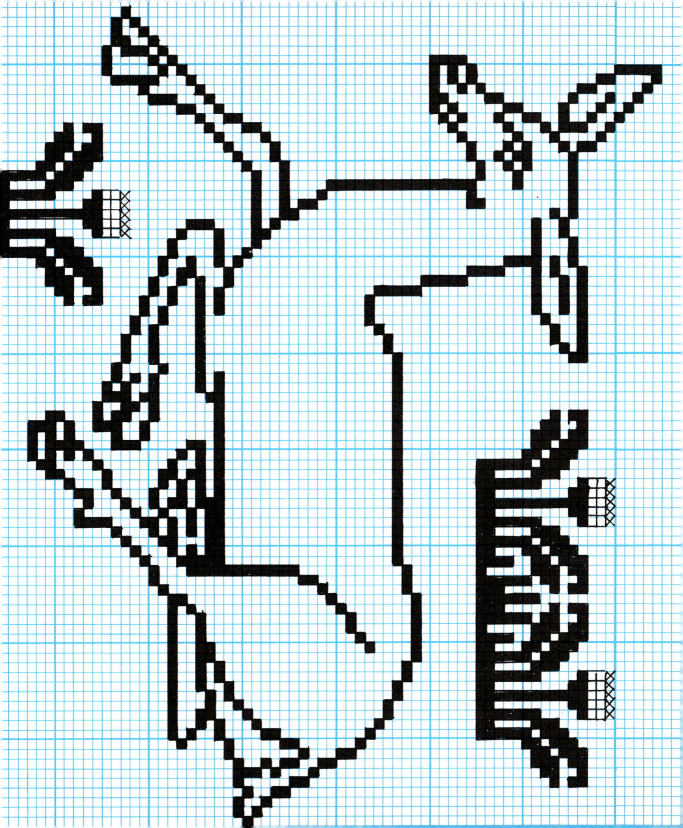

Cross stitches

Cross stitch is a fundamental stitch used in the majority of samplers and almost exclusively in the later ones. There are several ways of working it. Use a tapestry needle and work over a diagonal of two threads, or over one block of Aida, Binca or Bincarette.

A. A complete row of half crosses working from the right to left of the design and starting at the bottom of the stitch. The half stitches are then worked over again from left to right. The needle is always in a vertical position.

B and C. Each cross is completed before passing on to the next stitch. This makes a better shaped and a harder wearing stitch on canvas than method A. The needle position is alternately vertical and diagonal. It can be worked from right to left (B) or left to right (C). Modern technique demands that the stitches must be crossed in the same direction and that the top thread should always slope from the bottom left to the top right of the stitch. This is the recommended method for working cross stitch patterns, unless you are interested in doing reversible embroidery.

The cross stitches used on samplers throughout the seventeenth and eighteenth centuries were more complex and some are given here for embroiderers interested in historical accuracy. The Owl on the Vine sampler is worked in these stitches, which are completely reversible, but a little time consuming. Great care must be taken with starting and finishing. Leave a thread at the beginning and when the pattern is established, change to a crewel needle and carefully work the thread into the fabric.

As our ancestors left no sewing manuals behind them, short of undoing some of the work, some of their techniques must remain a matter for conjecture. Close study of samplers show that embroiderers evolved their own methods and that these differed from worker to worker.

D. Marking cross stitch. This presumably gets its name from its widespread use in marking linen. It is worked in three stages. After making the first double diagonal, the needle enters the centre of the stitch and comes out again at another corner, so making two half stitches, one on either side of the fabric. The second double diagonal is then made and the completed stitch is the same on both sides. The needle is always in a diagonal position. With a little practice reversible designs can be worked because the direction the needle takes after it enters the centre of the stitch is adaptable to the needs of the design.

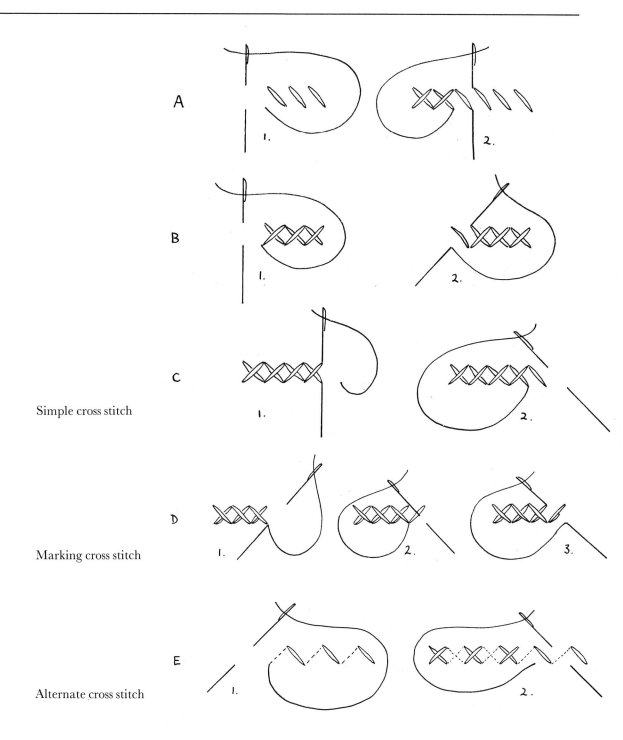

A

B

C

Simple cross stitch

D

Marking cross stitch

E

Alternate cross stitch

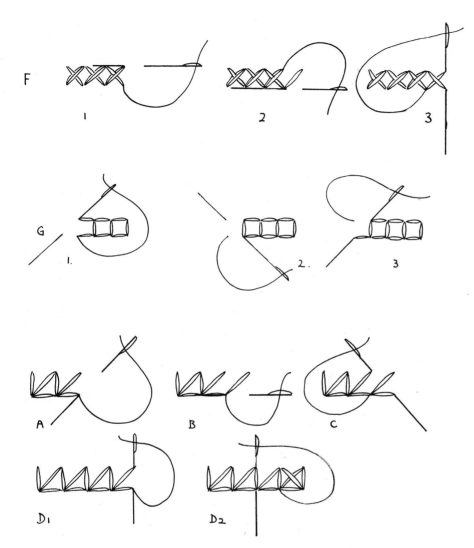

F

1   2   3

Cross stitch reversible to four-sided stitch

G

1.   2.   3

Four-sided stitch reversible to cross stitch

A   B   C

D1   D2

Two-sided Italian cross stitch

This is an interesting stitch to work, but in following a design it is not always possible to make the top diagonals flow from the bottom left to the top right of the stitch. This was of less importance to our ancestors than it is to us. It is easier to work this stitch in a frame than in the hand, though whether or not to use a frame must be a matter for personal preference.

E. Alternate cross stitch. This is worked in two journeys and the needle is always in a diagonal position. Work from right to left, making diagonals alternately on the front and back of the fabric. Finish the crosses on the return journey. This stitch was used extensively on simple borders (see Sampler 7) and also for working in two colours, first working a row in one colour and then filling in the alternate spaces in another colour. Trees and houses were often worked in this way.

F. Cross stitch reversible to four-sided stitch. This was used particularly in alphabets, the cross making the obverse and the square the reverse of the letters. Easy to work in a straight line, it is a very difficult stitch to use in complex lettering patterns, and in studying samplers one is amazed at the wonderful technique of the workers. Work from left to right and note that the first diagonal is worked over a second time. The needle is sometimes horizontal and sometimes vertical.

G. Four-sided stitch reversible to cross stitch. This stitch is not nowadays regarded as a cross stitch, but it is given here because of its use on samplers in relation to the other cross stitches. It is worked from right to left, in three stages. The needle is always in a diagonal position. The stitch is the reversal of F.

H. Two sided Italian cross stitch. This can be worked over a square of two or four threads each way. The method given here is worked in two journeys and is reversible.
(a) Make the diagonal, bringing the needle back into the same hole.
(b) Make the base line, bringing the needle back into the same hole.
(c) Make the upright, bringing the needle out at the right end of the base stitch, then make (a) again.
(d) Return journey. Insert the needle at the top of the diagonal and bring it out at the right end of the base stitch. Continue working backwards along the row to the beginning.

Sampler 2. The Three Pears

This sampler is made up from patterns taken from two samplers in the Victoria & Albert Museum, both dating from about the middle of the seventeenth century. Both are random samplers, the second signed with the initials P.B.

A variation border for working in oriental stitch

The one from which the pear pattern has been taken has in its top section seven groups of formalised flowers and fruits worked in rococo stitch, and interspersed with small geometric patterns in various stitches. Below are fourteen blocks of patterns, two featuring strawberries but the remainder being geometric. All are worked in silk, in oriental, rococo, rice and Algerian eye stitches. While the geometric patterns tend to cover the material completely, like modern canvas work, the flowers and fruits stand out freely from the linen background.

Some idea of the fineness of the work can be gained from the dimensions, which are 20 in. × 8 in. This is a little smaller than the sampler whose patterns are given below. It is not surprising then, that the geometric patterns have been a little simplified.

Rococo stitch has been neglected for many years, but seems to be gaining in popularity in modern canvas work, where its textured qualities are being appreciated. In the seventeenth century it was extremely popular, appearing in a large number of sampler patterns. It was used for making small personal items, like pockets and purses, some of which have survived. It is very easy to work in diagonal lines, and therefore it was very popular for working geometric patterns.

The Three Pears sampler is worked on Aida. This is a bold weave fabric which is ideally suited to the counting of threads. The holes between the blocks make for very easy working. It is available in various blocks counts.

Aida block count: 9 blocks to the inch.

Size of main designs: A. The pears, $7\frac{1}{4} \times 7\frac{3}{4}$ in.

E and F. The two diamonds, 4×4 in. each.

G. The base design, 5×8 in.

Thread: Anchor Soft Embroidery Cotton.

Overall size of material needed depending on the finish: (a) 23×12 in. (b) 25×14 in.

Size of finished sampler: $20\frac{1}{2}$ in. × 10 in.

To adapt the designs for other fabrics, see Chapter II, under Scale, oriental, rococo and rice stitches.

To prepare the material, see Chapter II, Method of Work.

Allow three or four inches at the top of the work, depending on your finishing technique.

Start with the top pear (A), the middle rococo stitch of the leaf being on the central tacking thread. The half stitches on each side of this arc made by working four straight stitches, fanning out from the base hole.

Work the two rows of diagonal rococo stitches (B), twelve in all, starting eight blocks on either side of the top of the pear leaf. The ends of these lines establish the edges of the sampler. It is now easy to fill in the areas of oriental stitch (C) eight blocks away from these diagonals, and the lines of oriental and cross stitches two blocks above (D). This minimises the chore of counting.

Work the next two pears.

Pattern E, in cross and rococo stitch is placed twenty four blocks below the first pear, aligned to the tacking thread.

Pattern F, in rice stitch is worked ten blocks below E.

Pattern G, in rice stitch is worked four blocks below F. Start on the central line and work outwards.

The placing of the square oriental stitch patterns (H) depends on whether you wish to include your initials and the date (see pages 84 and 108, for alphabet and numerals). If you decide to do this, they should fall into place between A and G in this way: four blocks free, seven blocks for initial, four blocks free, pattern H, four blocks free, seven blocks for a numeral, four blocks free.

Right. Patterns for sampler 2

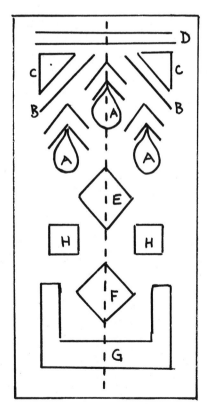

The layout for sampler 2

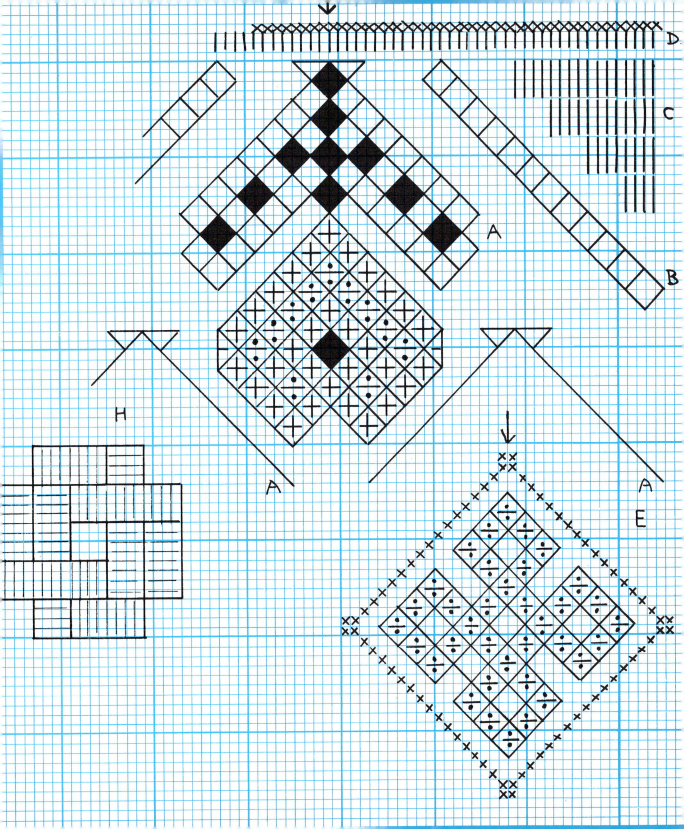

A

B

C

D

E

H

F

G

Pattern for sampler 2

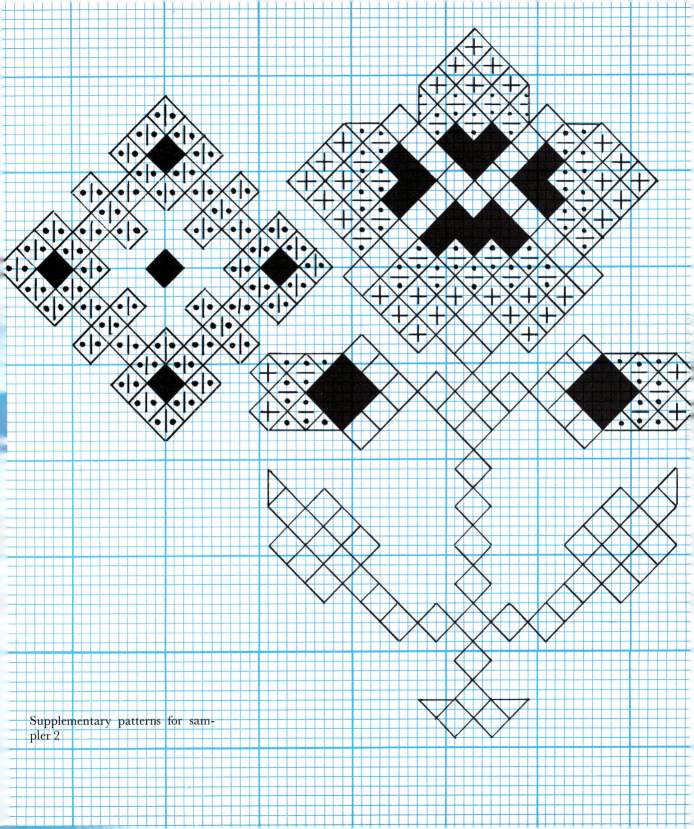

Supplementary patterns for sampler 2

For finishing, see Chapter VII.

Alternative designs using the same stitches are also given.

Oriental stitch

This is a straight stitch, worked in either horizontal or vertical lines, with one stitch going between each thread of the fabric. Use a thickness of thread to match the weight of linen, or the stitch will look sparse. It is usually worked over four threads, and always over an even number. Use a tapestry needle and work from right to left.

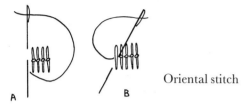

Oriental stitch

A. Starting at the bottom, make a straight stitch over four threads.

B. Bring the needle up to the left of this stitch, in the centre of the four fabric threads and secure it with a back stitch.

Rococo stitch

This is a variation of Oriental stitch, the stitches being grouped into clumps of four. Each starts and finishes in the same holes. The first straight stitch is pulled two threads to the right and held there by its back stitch. The two middle ones lie straight, and the last one is pulled two threads to the left. This makes a pleasing diamond shape. This stitch is easy to work diagonally when the hole made by the last back stitch of one clump becomes the head of the next group of four.

This may seem rather intimidating, but if Oriental stitch is learnt first it should not be difficult. Try working it on Binca or Aida fabric in the first instance, and you will find the positioning of the stitches easier.

When this stitch is worked on a linen scrim, holes develop at the top and bottom of each clump because of the pull of the stitches. These holes add a lacy texture to what is already a most distinctive stitch.

Rice stitch

Make a large cross stitch over a square of four threads each way. (See cross stitch B.) Each arm of the cross is then crossed in turn by a back stitch.

A. Bring the needle out in the space between the top diagonals and make a back stitch over the top right arm of the cross.

B. Work round the other arms, following the diagram.

Rococo stitch

Rice stitch

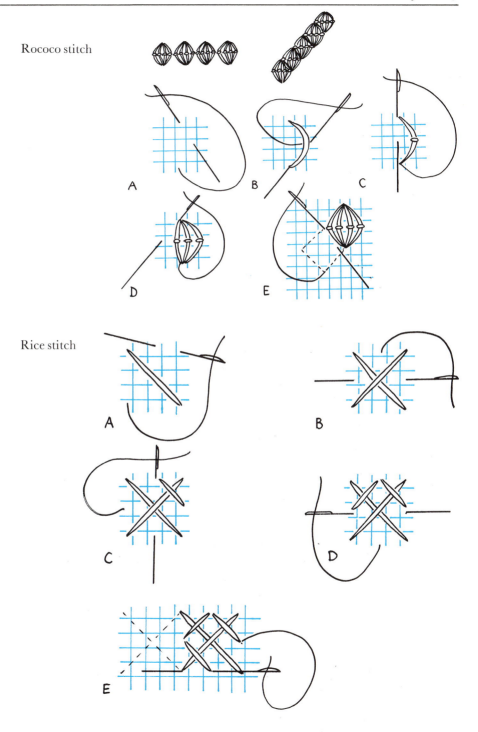

IV
THE GREAT AGE

Snail motif for random placement

It is easy to say that the sixteenth century sampler was of one type and that the seventeenth century sampler was of another, but the truth is not quite so convenient. The spot sampler of earlier times continued to flourish well into the new century, and was gradually superceded by new fashions. These held sway for seventy years and more, before being in their turn outmoded. Netherthless, the century as a whole is the great age for samplers. A large number have survived, often in excellent condition, and they show such vitality, such a range of stitch and pattern, such colour and amazing technique that they are a wonder and delight.

The seventeenth century in England saw the fine flower of the Renaissance in full bloom. Under the influence and patronage of Charles I not only great state buildings such as the Banqueting Hall in Whitehall were being erected, but many fine domestic buildings also. The Queen's House at Greenwich is a good example. After the exuberant but tough world of the Elizabethans, there was a tremendous increase in the elegancies and refinements of society. The century also saw an increase in the amount of personal wealth that was available to spend on these refinements.

Even the civil war, which made a permanent mark on our political life, was not a major disruptive influence in society as a whole, which through the century grew in richness and enjoyed a standard of domestic comfort such as had never been known before. The samplers of the seventeenth century reflect just one tiny facet of this happy state of affairs.

Though domestic taste was becoming more elegant and less ostentatious than in the previous century, it was still an age when men had limited outlets for the expression of their wealth and their position in society – and so they still wore their fortunes on their backs. Their clothes and the adornment of their homes afforded the conventional way by which men could express their wealth.

Flower motif for random placement

It follows that skill in needlework was a very desirable asset in a woman of any class, and a man who had the support of a well trained band of needlewomen was happy indeed. Girls were well grounded in embroidery as a matter of course. From Milton, writing in the middle of the century, we find that making a sampler was no longer the occupation of the wealthy or noble lady. It had become quite a humdrum domestic activity.

> "It is for homely features to keep home............
> .... coarse complexions
> And cheeks of sorry grain will serve to ply
> The sampler, and to tease the huswife's wool."

But higher up the social scale Evelyn the diarist describes his daughter as having 'an extraordinary genius for whatever hands can do with a needle,' and higher still, Queen Mary is reported as never travelling abroad in her carriage without some employment for her fingers (A. F. Kendrick, *English Needlework*).

During the century there was a tremendous increase in the number and type of books in circulation. Books, and particularly herbals, with any sort of illustration were sources of patterns for embroidery, but two pattern books in particular were published which had a considerable influence on embroidery and sampler making.

Above. Drawn thread ground with darned fillings (from a contemporary pattern book)
Right. Needlemade lace

33

The first, *A Schole-House, for the Needle* by Richard Shorleyker, published in 1624, consists of a fine collection of lace patterns, printed in white on black to give the full effect of the designs. Then follows various border patterns and 'sundry sortes of spots as will fitly serve to be wrought some with gould, some with silke, some with crewel in coullers.'

Another important book, *The Needle's Excellency*, was a reprint of a German pattern book by Sibmacher. In the 1640 edition in the Bodleian Library in Oxford, there is an engraving of a girl at work on her embroidery. At her feet is a small wicker work-box, and at the other side of her frame Cupid sits on a stool, working the sampler in the other direction. So far he has embroidered CUP. This book also contains a vast selection of patterns, largely for needlemade lace, and a delightful poem in praise of the needle by John Taylor.

> "A needle, though it be but small and slender
> Yet is it both a maker and a mender,
> A grave reformer of old Rents decayed
> Stops holes and seams and desparate cuts displayed."

In this book John Taylor also mentions various stitches by name. Ferne stitch, finny stitch, Queen stitch and Rosemary stitch leave us tantalised by our ignorance of their practical application.

Nothing reflects the truly domestic nature of the sampler better than the designs of which they are composed. The seventeenth century was an age when every child imbibed with its mother's milk a religious consciousness, yet the samplers are remarkable for the complete lack of overt religious symbolism in their designs. In the early years flowers, birds and animals (real and mythological) were worked in fine tent stitch, and beautifully shaded (Plate 1), but later in the century floral patterns were dominant. The medium in which they were worked (double running and cross stitches of all kinds), made for formalised drawing of the flowers, but they are clearly recognisable. Roses, honeysuckle, pansies, carnations, acorns, strawberries, grapes, thistles and daisies are all to be seen. It was an age in which gardens and gardening were important. Nature adorned the domestic scene without, and indoors formalised nature found its rightful place in domestic embroidery.

The sampler designs of the early years of the century reflect the fashions of the day. Garments decorated with double running stitch and black work patterns were still fashionable between 1620–1630, and some have survived. Bed hangings are more durable and some have survived to show the practical application of the spot patterns found in the samplers. These designs were worked on small squares of linen, cut out and appliquéd onto the hanging. In the Bodleian Collection there is an interesting sampler which shows birds, butterflies, a daffodil and a tulip already cut out from the linen and appliquéd to a satin ground with a metal couching thread.

Gradually the shape of the typical sampler changed from its earlier dimensions. It became a long strip, sometimes as narrow as six inches, and as long as a yard. It was obviously made from an off-cut of linen left over from some other purpose, for it was always a loom-width of fabric, with the selvedge running at the top and bottom, and the sides usually hem-stitched. It was intended to be kept rolled up on a wooden or ivory roller in a work-box. It continued to be worked in silks, but the use of sequins, beads or metal threads ceased. An amazing number of stitches were used, of which only a small selection of the most popular are used in the samplers in this book.

The spot motifs of the earlier work eventually died out, and strips or bands of patterns became dominant. Amongst these patterns, so predominately floral, there appears an enigmatic but amusing figure —the boxer (overleaf). Appearing in pairs facing each other and separated by foliage, these figures have puzzled embroidery historians as to their origin and meaning. The stance they invariably adopt is with one foot forward, and one arm raised. Their heads and shoulders are in the frontal position and they tend to look ferocious, largely because their features are worked in a continuous line of double running. Sometimes naked, sometimes wearing boots, or little running shorts, they usually carry a trophy, such as a sprig, a heart, or a flower.

Floral motif for use singly or as a border

Far left. A seventeenth centu⟨ry⟩
sampler with floral strip ⟨de⟩signs and boxes. Note t⟨he⟩
two 'boxers' at the top, sep⟨ar⟩ated by a clump of foliage.
*By courtesy of the Fitzwilli⟨am⟩
Museum.*

Left. Another seventeen⟨th⟩
century strip design, the flo⟨ral⟩
bands interspersed wi⟨th⟩
bands of lettering.
*By courtesy of the Victoria ⟨and⟩
Albert Museum.*

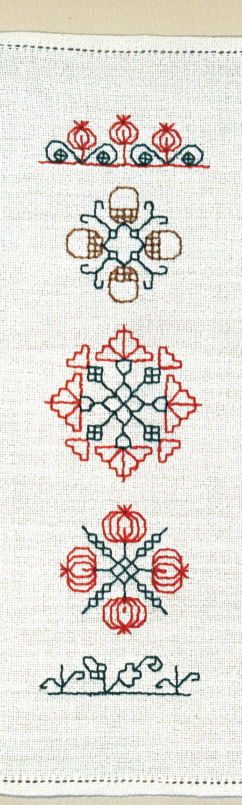

The Owl on the Vine

Acorns, Carnations and Pomegranates

The Three Pears

Blackwork

White Work

Acorns and Strawberries

Alphabets

Spring

Darning

Home and Abroad

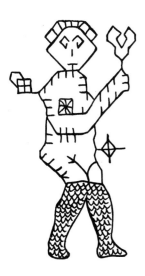

Small 'boxer' motifs in double running and detached buttonhole stitches

At one time thought to be an adaptation of Renaissance cupids, it is now thought that they are a corruption of designs current on the continent for many generations, in which two lovers approached a girl. In the design the girl has disappeared and become the foliage in between them, and the lovers have become stylised in these little figures (D. King).

Alphabets and numerals began to be included in samplers by the middle of the century, and work was often signed and dated. Experts think that from this time onwards samplers became increasingly the work of children, albeit very expert, rather than the work of adult needlewomen.

Some of the most magnificent samplers of the seventeenth century are those made in white work. This is a broad term used to cover a variety of types of work, but all executed on white (or during a brief period) yellow linen, and sewn in white linen thread. Only the very simplest forms of white work, that is block satin stitch designs with double running and detached buttonhole bars, and simple drawn thread work with needlework fillings, fall within the practical scope of this book. But so many examples of the much more difficult cut and drawn work with needlepoint fillings are to be seen in museums that it is worth attempting a brief description of the process by which they were made.

More boxers, rather fashionably dressed. The foliage between them was originally a maiden.

A large number of warp and weft threads were cut and drawn from the fabric to leave a grid of big holes separated from each other by a few remaining threads. New diagonal threads were put in and then these and the remaining threads of linen were all worked over with a fine linen thread in either needle-weaving or buttonholing to make them firm and strong.

On this open framework all sorts of patterns were built up, using a stitch similar to detached buttonhole stitch (page 61). A thread would be laid from one part of the framework to another and worked over, another thread laid and worked over, and so on. It was an extremely time-consuming process even for those days. To hold the work firm and make it possible to work a piece of vellum was tacked behind the linen. This was firm enough to hold the shape of the linen, but pliable enough to allow the needle to work. The Norwich Museum (Stranger's Hall) has a very interesting half-finished sampler which shows the threads withdrawn and the vellum in position.

On this grid consisting of squares and diagonals it was relatively easy to develop floral and geometric patterns, and even alphabets, but such was the virtuosity of the workers of the seventeenth century that they often chose subjects involving animals, birds and people. A very fine, very early sampler in the Museum of London shows the arms of Queen Elizabeth with lion and dragon supporting the shield, and with the royal cipher clearly legible around it (page 39). Judith, her maid, and the head of Holofernes (a most extraordinary choice of subject by any criterion) is not managed so successfully as the square grid distorts the proportions of the figures, making them more quaint than beautiful

Right. A satin stitch border
Left. Floral lace built up on horizontal bars

An early white work sampler, with the arms of Queen Elizabeth I clearly visible. The top two sections are worked with metal threads.
By courtesy of the Museum of London.

(The Fitzwilliam Museum, Cambridge). Mermaids were another favourite choice, with high coronets on their heads and long strands of linen hair falling down to their tails. One of the finest figures is that of Neptune (in the unfinished sampler at Norwich). He has a free flowing beard, a fine frill of lacy seaweed around his body, while on the upper side of his tail are the most wonderful detached curling scales.

In some samplers the grid of supporting threads has been entirely cut away, and the whole area filled with a scene worked freely in lace stitches. In these the figures are joined together with little bars and picots, and because the rigid geometric grid is not there the proportions of the figures are more successfully managed. The Fitzwilliam Museum has a beautiful example of this free lace filling, depicting firstly Adam and Eve driven from the Garden of Eden by the Angel with the flaming sword, and secondly Abraham and Sarah receiving the angels. They all wear seventeenth century dress. Abraham has a fine cloak and hat, and in the background is a charming tent with open flaps.

It is not surprising to learn that white work was regarded as the second stage in a child's needlework education. A long strip sampler might often be half and half, with ordinary coloured work at the top, and the bottom done in white work, often re-signed and with a later date. Martha Eldin, a rare example of a child whose education in embroidery is well annotated, made her coloured sampler at the age of eight in 1668 and her white work one a year later.

It is difficult to overestimate the place needle-made lace held in the fashion scene in the first half of the seventeenth century. Visitors to the Tate Gallery in London may be familiar with the delightful picture of the Saltenstall family, painted by David des Granges. Lady Saltenstall has just been brought to bed. She wears a lace cap and collar and the sheets of the bed have deep lace edges. The baby, in swaddling bands trimmed with lace, is nursed by a lady also wearing a deep lace collar. Sir Richard has narrow lace trimming on his collar and cuffs, and the two little children whom he is leading by the hand wear caps, collars, cuffs and aprons trimmed in the same way.

Makers of white work samplers were probably never expected to make such amazing quantities of lace, which must have been imported from Italy and the Low Countries. Nevertheless, as adults they would have the care and mending of lace, and probably produced narrow edging laces for clothes, at any rate for the baby. Even this was a very time-consuming business.

Styles in fashion and in fashionable embroidery changed very much before the end of the century. The great craze for lace declined, and it is not to be seen in the work of Lely, who was painting portraits at the close of the century. Many new influences were at work as a result of England's expanding horizons. Trade with the Far East began the fashion for Chinoiserie, which brought new designs into the domestic scene. These new ideas find no place in samplers, whose design content remained unchanged. Thus, what had at the beginning of the century been a reflection of contemporary taste had now become an academic exercise in learning needlework techniques. These techniques were brilliantly taught, and as brilliantly executed, but they do not reflect the climate of taste prevailing at the end of the century.

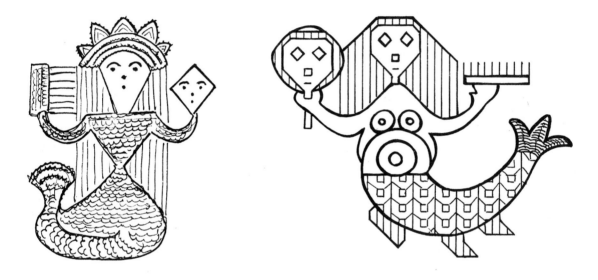

Far left. A lace mermaid with comb and mirror
Above. Another mermaid, in satin and double running stitches

One more floral motif, for working in satin, detached buttonhole and double running stitches

Sampler 3. Acorns, Carnations and Pomegranates

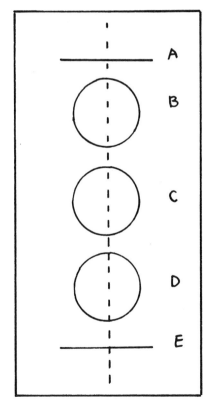

Layout for sampler 3

This work is composed of patterns taken from samplers in the Victoria and Albert Museum. It is made up of true double running patterns and therefore it should be possible to work it so that the sampler is completely reversible. This should not be too difficult because the fruit and flowers are worked in different colours from the framework of the patterns. This means that the first step in the analysis of the designs has been done for you, and they are already broken down into manageable sections. If you are a novice, do not attempt them without trying the double running stitch exercises (page 44). These patterns may also be worked in back stitch.

For adapting the design to other fabric counts see Chapter II, Scale, double running stitch.

Above. Patterns for sampler 3

Below. Extra double running stitch
borders and motifs, for substitution
as variations in sampler 3

Two more double running stitch borders

For preparing the fabric, see Chapter II, Method of Work.

Fabric count: 27 threads to the inch.

Size of main patterns: B. $1\frac{3}{4}$ in. square
C. $2\frac{1}{4}$ in. square
D. $2\frac{1}{4}$ in. square.

Thread: Clarks stranded cotton, two threads.

Overall size of material needed:

(a) 13 in. by 6 in. for a hemstitched edge.

(b) 14 in. by 7 in. for a mounted picture.

Size of finished work: $10\frac{3}{4}$ in. by $4\frac{1}{4}$ in.

Begin to work $2\frac{3}{4}$ in. or $3\frac{3}{4}$ in. down from the top of the fabric, depending on your choice of finishing. Start the design on the central tacking line.

Pattern A. Begin with the central pomegranate and work up the stem. Remember to complete the fruit before working down the stem. Now work to the far right, then to the far left. You should finish back in the middle of the border, with the fruits and base line complete. Add the branches in another colour.

Pattern B. Start at the top of the central acorn, leaving nine threads between it and A. Work the framework of the pattern in another colour, starting and returning to the base of the acorn you have just made. Remember to finish each tendril in turn. Finally, work the remaining acorns.

Repeat this method for pattens C, D and E, leaving nine threads between the patterns, and aligning the top central flower in each case with the central line of tacking.

For finishing, see Chapter VII.

Here are also included a selection of true double running stitch patterns, of a variety of complexity.

Double running stitch

Double running stitch is a basic stitch of English linen embroidery and is seen in the majority of samplers of the seventeenth and eighteenth centuries.

It is a deceptively easy-seeming stitch, but in fact it requires great concentration and analytical skill to work it successfully. In tackling a pattern, it is often best to start at a central point and work out first in one direction, establishing the basic line of the pattern. On returning to the starting point the details of the design are all filled in. Then work out in the other direction.

The difficulty lies in making sure that no part of a complex pattern is left out. The needle travels twice over the same ground, neither more

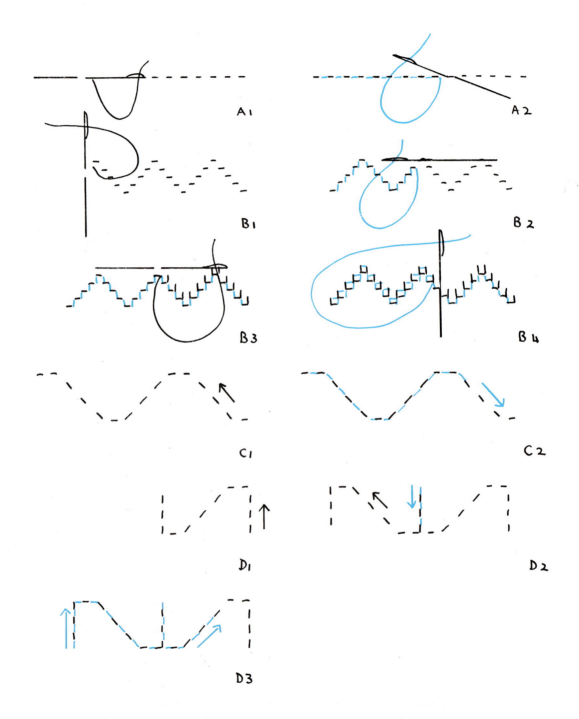

A 1

A 2

B 1

B 2

B 3

B 4

C 1

C 2

D 1

D 2

D 3

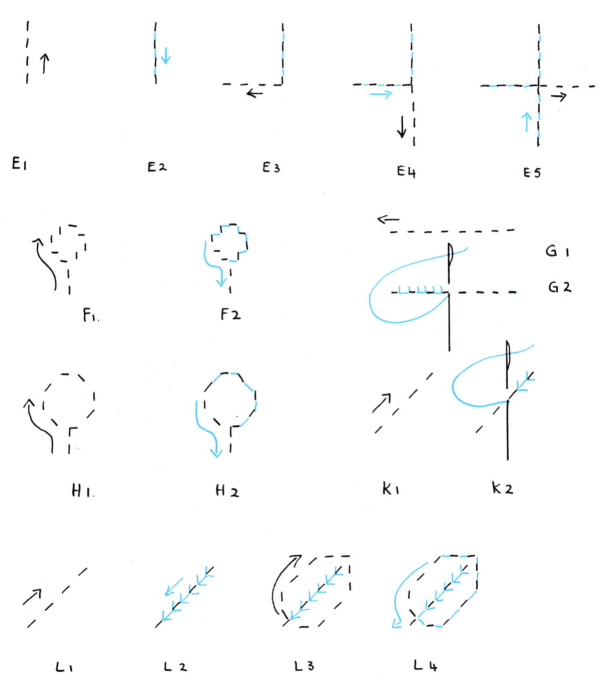

E1   E2   E3   E4   E5

F1.   F2   G1   G2

H1.   H2   K1   K2

L1   L2   L3   L4

Double running stitch exercises. Work the exercises in sequence from A to N if you are a novice, then you should be well equipped to tackle any of the double running patterns given in the book

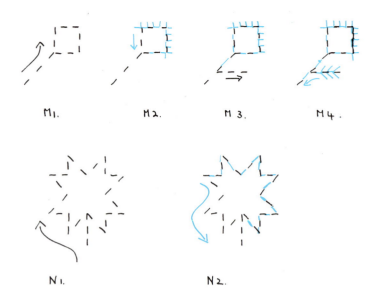

M1.   M2.   M3.   M4.

N1.   N2.

Left. Double running stitch exercises continued
Below. One more double running stitch border

nor less, and a pattern, when successfully completed, should be exactly the same on both sides of the fabric.

Double running stitch creates designs which have a wonderful clarity of line, reminiscent of the finest printing. It is worth a struggle to master its difficulties. It is possible for double running designs to be worked in back stitch, but the finished work is by comparison rather clumsy and does not compare with the beauty and lightness of a perfectly worked design in double running stitch.

Before embarking on any of the designs in this book the beginner will find it rewarding to work the exercises above. Try them first on Binca or Aida, where the blocks of threads and holes will help you. The straight and diagonal stitches will be easy to find and you will be able to concentrate on working the patterns. When you have mastered this, try the exercises on linen.

Use a tapestry needle. Leave a thread at the start and when the pattern has been established, work this invisibly into the linen, using a crewel needle.

A. Pick up and miss three threads of the fabric, or one block of Binca or Aida.

B. Work backwards over the line of running stitches, filling in the spaces. Slant the needle so that it enters at the top and exits at the bottom of the established stitches.

In the diagrams the black is the first journey and the blue is the second.

Sampler 4. Blackwork

The patterns for this sampler came from two sources, one in the Victoria and Albert Museum, and the other from the Fitzwilliam Museum, Cambridge.

Blackwork was a very popular type of embroidery, in high fashion during the Tudor period, and lasting into the first few decades of the seventeenth century. It is familiar to us through the paintings of Holbein who, employed by Henry VIII as a court painter, has given to posterity the finest record of fashion ever made. So associated is he with this particular style of embroidery that Holbein stitch is an alternative name for double running stitch. Visitors to the National Portrait Gallery can see the portrait of Catherine Howard, fifth wife of Henry VIII, painted by him. A delicate frilling of linen, finely embroidered with black patterns, surrounds her wrists, and makes a perfect foil for the dark, rich heaviness of her dress. In the Victoria and Albert Museum there is a fine linen shirt embroidered at the wrists and neck. The pattern is of columbines, and the stitch double running. Its approximate date is 1540.

Blackwork is sometimes referred to as Spanish work, and in the past Catherine of Aragon was credited with introducing this embroidery into England. It is now thought that she encouraged a style already established here.

Blackwork is a type of monochrome embroidery not necessarily worked in black. The sixteenth century shirt is worked in blue, and there are many examples worked in red.

Blackwork patterns took two main forms. Strip patterns, either of stylised flowers or geometric forms were used for the adornment of personal linen, as in the portrait mentioned above. There is a tremendous number and variety of these to be found in samplers, and they retained their popularity long after the fashion for wearing garments decorated with them had disappeared. An example of this is the two strip patterns at the base of this sampler. They date from the eighteenth century and therefore were definitely old fashioned at the time they were sewn.

Secondly, there were the all-over scroll-like patterns, with leaves and flowers breaking from curving stems with interlacing tendrils. These were worked in strong outline stitches like chain or stem stitch, and sometimes in an interlacing braid stitch using silver thread. The insides of the leaves and petals were filled with diaper patterns, that is small geometric shapes repeated across the surface of the fabric. Worked in either back or double running stitches they filled the shapes with varying densities of colour. This type of work was used for whole garments, such as jackets, coifs, caps and insets in the fronts of dresses. There are a few extant samplers which give a good range of these diaper patterns. Some of them can be seen here embroidered within shapes which show how they were originally intended to be used. The great charm of this particular type of embroidery depends on

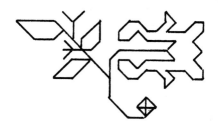

A blackwork columbine

Layout for sampler 4

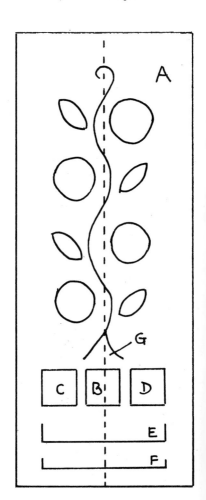

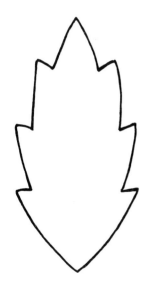

Leaf and pattern shapes

three things: its reversible quality, its clarity of line, and the amazing subtlety that can be achieved by varying the heaviness or lightness of the diaper fillings. This is done in two ways; firstly by using patterns with either close or sparse stitchery, and secondly by varying the weight and type of thread used in the work. The following sampler tries to show these three qualities.

Count of linen: 32 threads to the inch.

Size of designs: A. $12\frac{1}{2} \times 5$ in.

                B, C, D. 2×2 in.

                E. $6\frac{1}{2} \times 1\frac{1}{4}$ in.

                F. 7×1 in.

Thread: DMC Coton à broder Nos 18 and 25. Danish Flower Threads or Black Sewing Cotton No. 40 or 50.

Overall size of material:

    (a) 23×12 in.

    (b) 25×14 in. depending on type of finish.

Size of finished work: 21×10 in.

To adapt the design to other types of fabric, see Chapter II, under Scale, double running stitch.

To prepare the linen, see Chapter II, Method of Work.

Draw a curving line approximately twelve inches long on tracing or domestic greaseproof paper (see diagram and illustration, page 47 and opposite). On either side of the curving line trace the leaf and flower shapes four times. They should be opposite to each other and alternating in position, about half an inch apart horizontally, and an inch apart vertically. Splay out the end of the curved line, like the base of a tree.

Pin the paper carefully to your linen with the central tacking thread running down through the curve.

Allow 8 or 9 inches of fabric below the end of the tracing for the rest of the design.

With small stitches, tack the paper to the fabric through all the traced lines. If you use a fine black cotton for this, the tacking stitches will be hidden beneath your completed embroidery, and need not be removed.

When the tacking is complete, remove the pins, and carefully tear the paper away. The top part of your sampler is now ready to sew.

Outline all the shapes and the tree stem with either chain or stem stitch (page 53). Use a thicker thread for the flowers and a finer thread for the leaves. (DMC Coton à broder Nos. 18 and 25.)

Work the diaper patterns inside the shapes, using a fine thread for all the fillings (Danish Flower Thread or Fine Sewing Cotton No. 50).

G

B

C

D

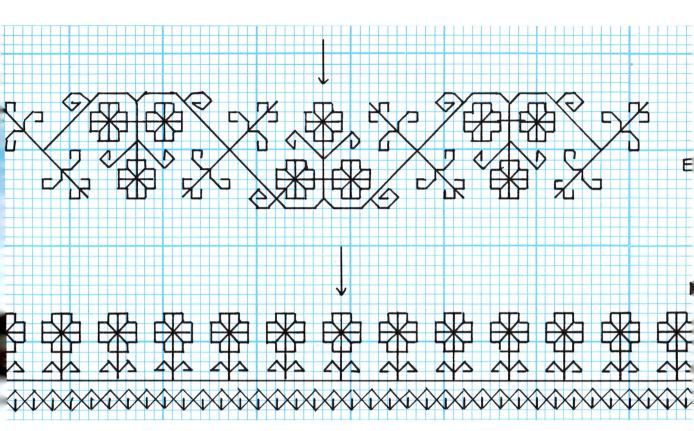

E

Choose lighter designs for the leaves and heavier designs for the flower fillings.

In the base of the tree use filling G using a fine thread at the top and a coarser thread below. To vary the weight of the embroidery always choose a coarser thread, rather than doubling a fine thread in the needle. This makes a cleaner, better-shaped stitch.

Because the individual shapes that make up diaper patterns are so small it is hardly worth working them in double running stitch. Back stitch is more satisfactory for this purpose (page 53).

It is a good idea to begin the work in the centres of the shapes where the patterns are complete, and to work outwards to the sides where the shapes are often broken into by the outline.

When the tree is complete, work pattern B in double running stitch (page 44). Start sixteen threads or $\frac{1}{2}$ in. below the tree, the centre aligned to the central tacking thread. Use a fine thread and start by the centre mark.

Work patterns C and D on either side. Leave sixteen threads between them and B. These patterns are difficult, and simpler ones can

Left and above. Patterns for the blackwork, sampler 4

51

Left. Alternative designs for black-work samplers, which may be worked in double running or back stitch

be substituted if required (see opposite). Alternatively they can be omitted altogether and the sampler finished off with patterns E and F.

Leave sixteen threads or half an inch below B and work E and F, in each case from the central point. Work F in a heavier thread.

To make up, see Chapter VII.

Back stitch

Back stitch

This stitch can be used as an outline stitch, or in making black work patterns. For the latter, use a tapestry needle.

Work from right to left.

Bring the needle through the fabric a stitch-length from the start. Go backwards the length of the stitch and bring the needle forward the length of the next stitch. On the back of the work it looks like stem stitch.

Stem stitch

Stem stitch

A useful stitch for outlining shapes often filled by other stitches. Use a crewel needle.

Work from left to right.

Keep the thread below, to the right of the needle.

Make a small stitch backwards towards the starting thread, the needle slanting upwards a little. Each stitch overlaps its predecessor by half its length.

Chain stitch

A useful stitch used for outlining shapes or for adding details to flowers in some early samplers. Use a crewel needle and work towards you.

Bring the needle to the right side of the work.

A. Insert the needle in the same place, to make a small running stitch.

B. Pass the thread behind the needle before pulling it through.

Chain stitch

Sampler 5. Acorns and Strawberries

The designs which make up this sampler are typical of seventeenth century work. These come from the Victoria and Albert Museum, London, but popular designs were copied again and again, and in fact patterns C and D can also be seen in the Fitzwilliam Museum, Cambridge (see Plate 3).

Both acorns and strawberries are recurring themes in sampler designs. They appear both as spot and strip designs, and it is fascinating to study them worked in various media. The strawberry is usually more true to life, with flower, berry and leaf clearly recognisable. Acorns are unmistakeable, but true oak leaves are rarely to be seen.

Though the basic outline of the designs are here worked in double running stitch, these patterns are of a different type from those in Sampler 4.

Many strip designs have a strong geometric line running through them, can best be described as an alternating V-shape. The point of the V is cut away, so making a flat base. From the centre of the base comes a design of stylised flowers and foliage, which is alternately rising or falling according to whether the V from which it springs is upright or inverted. A close study of page 36 will show a number of strip patterns in this basic shape. This shape is not confined to English embroidery patterns, but can be seen in linen embroideries right through Europe, and in carpet patterns from the Middle East.

Amazing variety is given to this shape by altering the proportions of the base and sides. Sometimes the sides develop into interesting coils and plaits. The acorns and strawberries from pattern D have sprung from a knot in the centre of a side, and the main part of the design (a rose) is not shown. Pattern E has coiled sides, and if the design were to be continued, the floral spray with acorns would be inverted. Pattern F shows another treatment of a side, where its shape is modified by introducing a vertical plait in its centre (this shape can be seen in simplified form in the border on Sampler 10).

In the seventeenth century these strip designs were worked in a good variety of coloured silks, and a large repertoire of stitches.

The outlines of many designs were worked either in very fine Montenegrin cross stitch or two sided Italian cross stitch, worked diagonally. These were virtuoso performances frequently achieved by

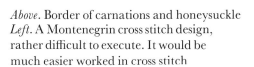

Above. Border of carnations and honeysuckle
Left. A Montenegrin cross stitch design, rather difficult to execute. It would be much easier worked in cross stitch

the workers of the seventeenth century, but not to be attempted lightly by the lesser mortals of the twentieth!

In the sampler, the main stitch is double running stitch, with filling stitches of satin, running, detached buttonhole, oriental and chain stitches, all of which are typical of the period.

Count of linen: 32 threads to the inch.

Size of designs: A. 5 in. × $\frac{3}{4}$ in.

B. 5 in. × 3 in.

C. $2\frac{3}{4}$ in. × $1\frac{3}{4}$ in.

D. $2\frac{3}{4}$ in. × 3 in.

E. $7\frac{1}{4}$ in. × $2\frac{1}{2}$ in.

F. $\frac{1}{2}$ in. × $10\frac{3}{4}$ in.

G. 1 in. × $\frac{3}{4}$ in. repeated 14 times.

Thread: Anchor Pearl Cotton No. 8.

Overall size of material needed:

(a) 19 × 12 in.   or

(b) 21 × 14 in. depending on type of finish.

Size of finished work: $17\frac{1}{4}$ × $9\frac{1}{2}$ in.

To adapt the design to other types of fabric, see Chapter II, under Scale, double running stitch.

To prepare the linen, see Chapter II, Method of Work.

A, B, C, D and E are easy to place on the fabric, starting in each case with the central tacking thread aligned to the central point of the design.

Begin border A, at the point marked, allowing three and a half or four and a half inches at the top of your fabric depending on your choice of finish. Work in double running stitch (page 44). The acorn cups are worked in detached buttonhole stitch (page 61).

B, C, D and E fall into place below this border. Allow half an inch or fifteen threads between the bottom of one pattern and the top of the one below. Start working from the top in each case.

B is worked in double running stitch, with a single running stitch (over three, under three) filling in the berries and the centre of the flower.

C is worked in double running stitch throughout.

D is worked in a framework of double running stitch, with a single running stitch (over three, under three) down the diagonals. The acorns, the flower centres, and the central knot are filled in with block satin stitch (page 61).

The acorn cups and the strawberries are filled in with detached buttonhole stitch.

The detail on the flower is in chain stitch (page 53).

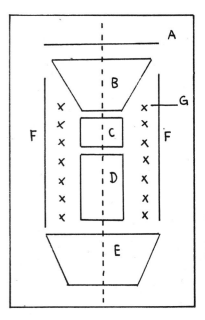

Layout for sampler 5

Patterns for sampler 5

A

C.

G

E

This page, B, D and F, patterns for sampler 5.

Some more complex
patterns and borders for inclusion
in sampler 5 if required

E is worked in double running stitch, with a single running stitch down the coiled sides and base.

The tiny acorns and cups are filled in with block satin stitch.

The big acorns and the flower centre are worked in detached buttonhole stitch.

The acorn cups are filled in with oriental stitch (page 30).

F is worked in double running stitch. Start at the bottom of the pattern, its base point aligned with the sides of E (see diagram).

G. The little strawberry plants are worked in double running stitch and the berries filled in with a single running stitch (over two, under two). They need to be accurately placed in relation to F, and to each other. Place the bottom one on each side with its central point twenty-four threads or three quarters of an inch from the side of F. It is then easy to place the rest in relation to the first, each nine threads above the last, seven strawberries in all.

A number of other acorn designs are given. They are of varying degrees of difficulty, but if they are analysed carefully should not prove impossible.

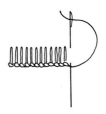

Buttonhole stitch

Buttonhole stitch

This stitch was used widely in white work to outline the areas for drawn fabric embroidery or needle-made lace. The area to be enclosed can be outlined with a small running stitch, which if done carefully, will help you to count the threads for this. It will also strengthen the edge.

Work from left to right, using a tapestry needle. Make each stitch over the same number of threads, one stitch lying between each fabric thread. Insert the needle at the head of the stitch. Bring it out at the bottom and put the thread behind the needle before pulling it through.

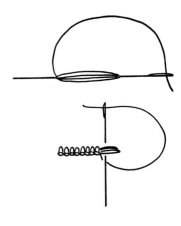

Buttonhole bars

These were used widely in white work designs and added a wonderfully rich texture to the work.

A. Make three straight stitches on top of each other over six or nine fabric threads, the needle entering and exiting from the same space each time.

B. Then proceed as for buttonhole stitch, working over the straight stitches and not entering the fabric at all.

C. To make a petal, turn the work and make three more straight stitches, using the same holes again. Work over with buttonhole stitch. The two bars force each other into a slight curve, so making the petal.

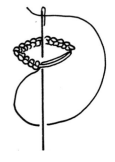

Buttonhole bars

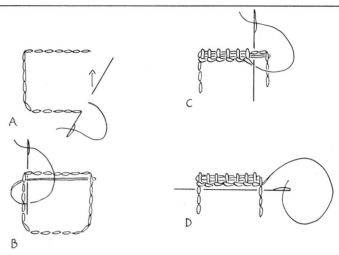

Detached buttonhole stitch

A

B

C

D

Detached buttonhole stitch

This was the basic stitch used in the needle-made lace patterns which form the most exciting part of white work samplers. In the examples given in this book it is only used as a filling stitch, for which purpose it was also very popular.

A. Outline the shape to be filled with either double running or back stitch, finishing the stitch at a convenient top corner of the shape.

B. Bring the needle to the front of the work and lay a thread across the top of the shape, by threading the needle through a stitch on the opposite side.

C. Now work buttonhole stitch, enclosing this thread, into the line of prepared back stitches along the top. At the end of the row, run the needle through a back stitch, lay it across the work again and proceed with the buttonhole stitch. When you reach the bottom, the buttonhole stitch is worked into the base line of back stitches.

Note that none of the buttonhole stitches goes into the background fabric and that they are always worked in the same direction across the area to be filled in.

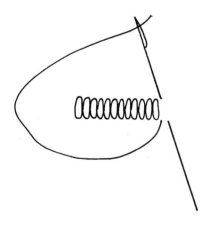

Block satin stitch

Block satin stitch

Use a tapestry needle and match the thickness of thread to the weight of the fabric to prevent the work looking sparse. Work from the bottom to the top of the stitch, taking care always to work between the threads of fabric. Work in either horizontal or vertical bars, with one thread lying between each fabric thread.

The smooth beauty of this simple stitch is used to complement the other more intricately textured white work stitches.

Sampler 6. White Work

Only the simpler types of embroidery found in seventeenth century white work samplers have been included in this piece.

These are patterns for block satin stitch with double running stitch, buttonhole bars with double running stitch and simple drawn thread work with needlepoint or darning fillings. Very many samplers contain examples of all three types, and designs for the third can be found also in *A Schole-House for the Needle*, and *The Needle's Excellency*.

Though we have a great deal of knowledge about how the elaborate needlepoint lace designs were used, the same cannot be said of these three types. This would seem to be because they were not fashionable enough to be recorded in the portraits and paintings of the day. They are of a kind of embroidery suitable for household linen, and one may assume that they were used in this way, and that in the ordinary course of events the linen has been worn out and discarded.

In the seventeenth century pattern books the filling inside the woven bars is drawn as an upright cross with a knot at its centre. Mrs Christie in *Samplers and Stitches* describes this knot as being very difficult to achieve, and depending on an exactly correct relationship between the size of the hole to be filled and the thread for working the stitch. The children who worked these designs on samplers would have agreed with her, and for the most part the needlepoint filling that they used was much simpler. This, known as dove's eye filling, is used here.

The designs are all part of band patterns. The diamond shapes (C and E) would be repeated along a line, with triangular shapes filling in to make a straight band, and pattern G is a half-section of a pattern which would itself enclose diamond shapes if it was repeated along a band. The sampler shape echoes the long strip sampler of the seventeenth century.

Linen count: 21 threads to the inch.

Size of designs: A. $6 \times 3\frac{1}{4}$ in.

B. $6 \times 1\frac{3}{4}$ in.

C. $6 \times 5\frac{1}{2}$ in.

D. 6×3 in.

E. $6 \times 5\frac{3}{4}$ in.

F. $6 \times 3\frac{1}{2}$ in.

G. $7\frac{1}{2} \times 4\frac{3}{4}$ in.

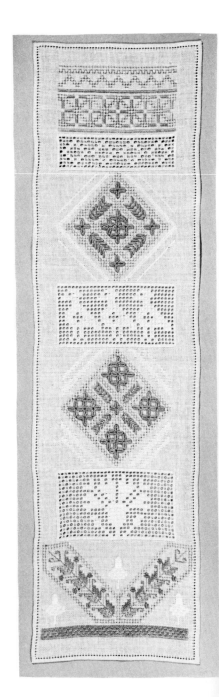

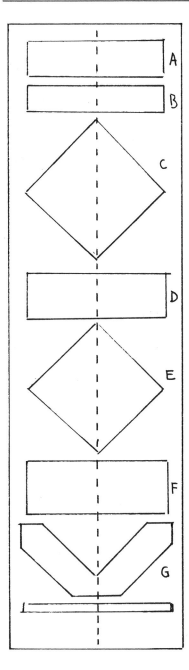

Layout for sampler 6

Thread: Anchor Pearl No. 5 for buttonholing, satin, double running and darning. Anchor Pearl No. 8 for whipped bars. Sewing Cotton No. 50 for dove's eyes.

Colour: The threads used in the drawn thread work should match the colour of the linen.

Overall size of material:

    (a) 33 in. $\times$ 10 in.   or

    (b) 35 in. $\times$ 12 in. depending on the finish you prefer.

Size of finished sampler: 31 in. $\times$ $8\frac{1}{2}$ in.

To adapt the designs to other fabrics, see Chapter II, under Scale, double running stitch, and drawn thread work.

To prepare the material, see Chapter II, Method of Work.

Allow $2\frac{1}{2}$ or 3 inches at the top of your fabric, depending on your choice of finish.

Begin to work chart A, starting at the central tacking thread. There are 43 stitches in all, 21 on either side of the central stitch, which spans the tacking thread. Work in double running stitch and block satin stitch.

Follow the charts carefully, leaving three threads only between each pattern, and starting always at the central tacking thread.

For B, D and F the plan adopted was to cut 1 thread and leave 3. (See drawn thread ground.)

B. Enclose 129 threads across and 33 threads down in a rectangle of buttonholing. This is $32 \times 4 + 1$, and will give you 32 bars and 33 holes across the work. You may find it easier to work the top line of buttonholing, cut and half draw out the central thread, and then work from either side of this. You will then have a central hole, with 16 holes and bars on either side of it. Then complete the buttonholing. Downwards work over 33 threads $(8 \times 4 + 1)$. This will give you 8 bars and 9 holes. Start by pulling the top thread.

    D. Across work as for B.

        Work downwards over 61 threads. This is $15 \times 4 + 1$ and will give 15 bars and 16 holes.

    F. Across work as for B.

        Work downwards over 69 threads. This is $17 \times 4 + 1$ and will give 17 bars and 18 holes.

To work the fillings follow the chart.

Patterns C, E and G alternate with these drawn thread patterns.

    C. Start 3 threads below B at the central point.

        Work in double running stitch and buttonhole bars.

    E. Start 3 threads below D at the central point.

        Work in double running, block satin and buttonhole bars.

A

B

F

G

Patterns for sampler 6

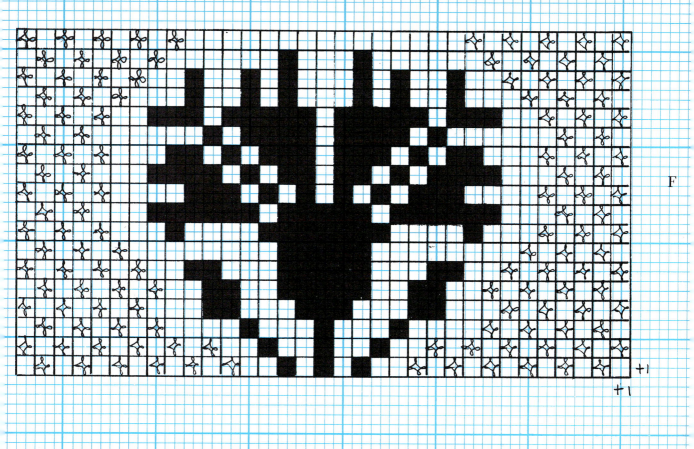

F

+1
+1

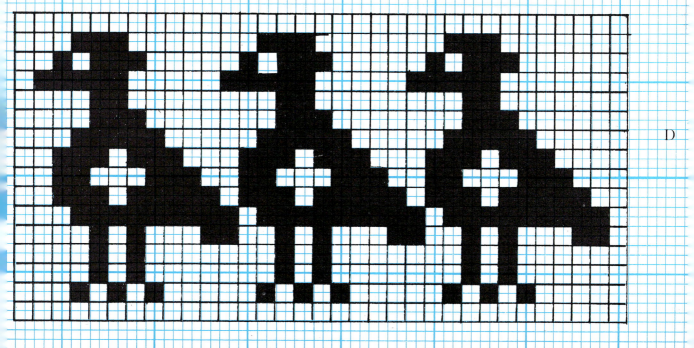

D

C

E

Patterns for sampler 6

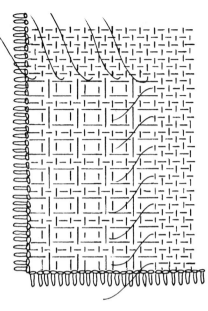

Drawn thread ground

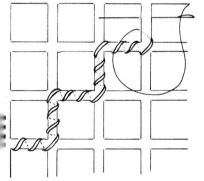

Overcast bars

G. Start 3 threads below F, 9 threads in from the side of F. (See chart).

Work in block satin, double running and stem stitch with buttonhole bars.

Drawn thread ground

The grid on which the drawn thread designs are worked is made by first enclosing the area with an edge of buttonhole stitch (see page 60). The number of threads to be enclosed must be counted carefully, and depends on the pattern of cutting and leaving threads which you wish to adopt. If you decide to cut two threads and leave two threads across the area, you must count any multiple of four threads, plus two. This is the conventional way. If you decide to cut one thread and leave three across the area you must count a multiple of four threads plus one.

By removing two threads you get a thinner bar, but the fabric gets very floppy and can be more difficult to manage while you are doing the overcasting. By removing only one thread you get a thicker bar, but it is definitely easier for a novice to manage.

Work first across, and then down the enclosed area. Starting by the buttonhole edge, cut and pull out the first thread. Leave three, cut and pull one, and so on. This is not difficult if you use a firm, light touch and are working on a good evenweave linen. If you have counted correctly the finished grid will begin and end with a hole.

Overcast bars

When the necessary threads have been withdrawn, the linen is rather loose and floppy. It must be firmed up by whipping over the remaining threads.

Use a thread to match the weight and colour of the fabric and secure it into the back of the buttonholing.

Using a stem stitch action (page 53) work two or three stitches over each section. Pass over the intersection to the next part, pulling your embroidery thread firmly. It is best to work this diagonally, starting in the top left hand corner of the work, and zig-zagging up and down the area until all the bars are overcast. Use a tapestry needle.

Dove's eyes

This stitch makes a delicate filling for the square holes made by the overcast bars. It is important to use a thread the same colour as your linen, as it must travel invisibly behind the work from hole to hole. Experiment with the type of thread you need. A finer rather than a coarser thread will be more satisfactory as the finished effect must be lacy. An ordinary sewing cotton is often what is needed.

Secure the thread into the back of the work and bring it to the front in the middle of the top bar of a square. With a buttonhole action (page 60) make a stitch either into or over the bars of each side of the square in turn. Secure the last stitch with a little back stitch, before working the needle through the back of the work, to emerge in the correct position for filling the next square.

If the work is rather fine, the use of a crewel needle will facilitate the passage of the thread behind the work.

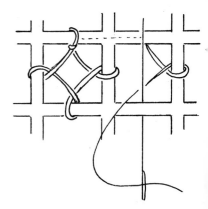

Dove's eyes

Darned filling

This filling makes the solid part of a pattern which shows up with great effect against the remaining open-work. Use a thread to match the linen and of a good weight to block in the design. Secure the thread in the back of a bar, and bring it to the front. Weave the needle under and over the bars sufficient times to block in the pattern. Travel behind the work to the next section to be blocked in.

This is very quick and easy to do.

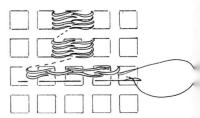

Darned filling

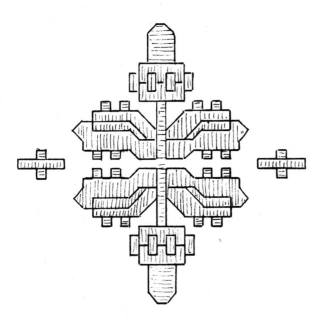

A block satin stitch motif

V
THE CONVENTIONAL SAMPLER
1700–1850

It was not until the eighteenth century that the sampler took the form which expresses everybody's idea of what a sampler should be. Of course long strip samplers continued to be made for some time, but soon new ideas developed, and a new type of sampler evolved which was different in form and content from what had gone before. When this new form had been established it was to remain the pattern, with minor variations, for about one hundred and fifty years. It was in fact to be the final form in the evolution of the sampler, and when it ceased to be made in the second half of the nineteenth century, it had fulfilled its function and the need for its making at that time no longer existed.

The new shape of the sampler was both shorter and wider than the old strip sampler. Its dimensions varied considerably, but whatever its actual measurements were the proportions became that of a picture. The finished work was intended to be ornamental and was no longer designed to be rolled up and put away in a work box. The materials also varied. Linen continued to be used throughout the period, but during the first half of the eighteenth century a fine woollen canvas, or tammy cloth, was also popular. This was a material bought for the purpose, and can be distinguished by a blue thread which runs down the selvedge. Unfortunately it was attractive to moths, and many of the samplers worked on this material have been badly damaged and one may presume that a large number have perished. Later in the century samplers were sometimes worked on cotton, on satin, or on silk gauze. The embroidery threads used showed a greater variety also, silk and linen threads being joined by wool and cotton.

The differences in shape and material of the eighteenth as compared with the seventeenth century sampler are superficial, compared to the differences in their content. The technical excellence of the earlier century could only have been achieved by children subjected to a very narrow and exacting system of education. Whether this took place in a school or in the home, so many long hours must have been spent in the pursuit of this perfection that little time can have been left for anything else. On the other hand, the work of the eighteenth century conveys the impression that for an ordinary girl a good grounding in needlework was essential, but that the higher flights of brilliance were unnecessary. The standard of girls' education was not very high but in that age of enlightenment was becoming a little broader.

This relaxation from a more rigid system meant that during the eighteenth century there was a steady decline in the number of stitches used in samplers. In the middle of the period cross stitch, four-sided stitch, eyelet, Algerian eye, and double running stitch were still popular. By the end of the period cross stitch remained the sole survivor of what had once been an enormous repertoire of stitches. Complex band patterns and even the figures of boxers occur in the middle of the century, but eventually they disappeared, along with the cut and drawn white work of earlier times. Simple band patterns worked in cross stitch survived and became the border patterns of the new samplers, while the space enclosed was filled up with alphabets, inscriptions, flowers, trees and a wonderful variety of objects reflecting the domestic scene.

Below. Another pair of boxers. Once again, the maiden between them has developed into foliage. All double running stitch

In some ways it is true to say that for the serious student of embroidery the samplers of this period are less exciting than those of earlier times. From the point of view of the child's embroidery being a part of social history, these samplers are endlessly entertaining and informative. Viewed as embroideries in their own right they should be regarded as needlework pictures, which is in fact what they became.

When the stitching of samplers ceased to be an education in itself, the sampler provided the educationalist with the ideal medium for instruction in a wider range of knowledge. The practice of learning and stitching the alphabet, which had begun during the previous century, was to be a dominant feature of sampler making until they finally died out in the nineteenth century. (See Alphabet Sampler, page 78.)

This was soon followed by the inclusion of a text or moral precept – 'Zeal in a good cause will merit applause' or 'To wisdom's counsel lend an ear, true godliness to gain' are typical examples. In the eighteenth century long inscriptions became part of samplers and there is no doubt that parents and teachers seized this opportunity to ground their children in the tenets of religion. The Lord's Prayer and the Creed, either separately or side by side, were set in a small border in the centre of the work and perhaps surrounded by wreaths of flowers. The Ten Commandments, sometimes rendered into doggerel verse, were set out on tablets with semi-circular tops, reminiscent of the Tablets of the Law still to be seen painted on the walls of many country parish churches.

Later in the century verses from hymns became very popular. Hymns were themselves an eighteenth century phenomenon and the great Independent hymn writers, Isaac Watts and Philip Doddridge were influencing the adult generation with some of the greatest hymns ever to be written. Dr Watts was a great innovator in that in Divine Songs and Moral Songs he wrote specifically for children, with such titles as 'Solemn thoughts of God and Death', 'The Sluggard' and 'Heaven and Hell'. These verses jar our sense of what is a fitting subject matter for children but they remained popular for generations, and are not unknown today.

> "How doth the little busy bee
> Improve each shining hour
> And gather honey all the day
> From every opening flower."

Charles Wesley's work provided for the Methodists a finer choice of hymns. 'Jesu, Lover of my soul,' was a favourite, though not all its verses were worked at one time. Both the Independents and the

Methodists set up their own schools and the education provided there must have influenced children in their choice of religious inscriptions.

Verses from the Bible retained their popularity until the end of the sampler-making period. Some of the most famous examples are those worked by the Brontë sisters and still preserved in the Museum at Haworth Parsonage. We learn from Charlotte's letters in later life how the children spent each afternoon in their aunt's bedroom receiving this instruction in needlework.

What was excluded from samplers is as illuminating as what was included. Nursery rhymes are conspicuous by their absence, as not being edifying enough. Instead there is a great variety of moral verse. Here is an example used by Susannah Strutt in 1820.

> "Learn little maid, each useful Art
> Which may adorn thy youth.
> Learn to improve thy tender heart
> In Virtue, Grace and Truth.
> Shun every vice with studied care
> Each female folly flee
> That every grace that crowns the fair
> May all attend on thee."

More typical of the definitely morbid tone which runs through these inscriptions is:

> "My life's a narrow span
> A short, uncertain stay.
> And if I reach the age of man
> It soon will pass away."

and

> "When I can read my title clear
> To mansions in the skies
> I bid farewell to ev'ry fear
> And wipe my weeping eyes."

This sense of impending doom and of the transience of life is somewhat oppressive to our ear. These verses must be read in the context of the mortality rates in cities during the eighteenth and first half of the nineteenth centuries, where death was a frequent visitor. For example, when the three Brontë sisters worked their samplers in 1829–31, and Charlotte, the eldest surviving child was thirteen, their mother and two elder sisters (whose samplers may also be seen in Haworth Parsonage Museum) were already dead.

Other subjects than religious and moral education were taught by

Right. A typical eighteenth century sampler with a pious motto.
By courtesy of the Victoria and Albert Museum.

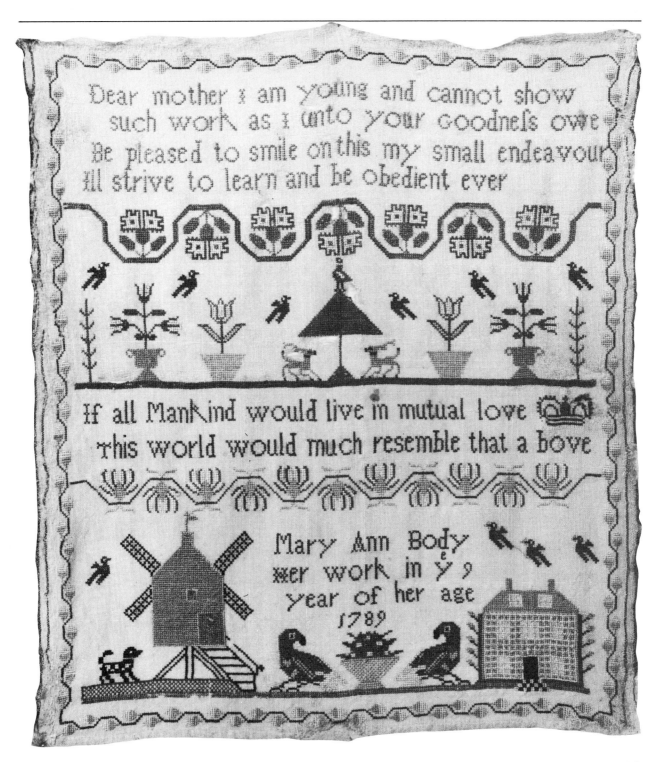

sampler making. Towards the end of the eighteenth century the making of map samplers became popular, particularly in the United States. Geography was at this time very much a matter of learning by rote, and by this method capes and bays were given some visual form. Calendar samplers were also popular, and in the Guildford Museum there is a long money sum. Worked in 1848 at St Matthew's School, £700,791–14–4 is divided by 1794.

Many asylums and schools are named on samplers, and sometimes the teacher's name. One, belonging to the National Federation of Women's Institutes is signed 'Sarah Hodgson, taught by Mary Wells at Bradford, 1765'. One signed Sophia Brunton 1799, and belonging to the Norwich Museum Collection, says 'A diligent scholar is an ornament to a school'. Even today the smug self-satisfaction of Sophia in being allowed to work this inscription is quite evident.

One of the charms of the samplers of this period is that they are not quite so anonymous as those of earlier years. Many museums have samplers which chronicle the marriage of a couple and the subsequent birth of their children. More melancholy are the mourning samplers, worked all in black and recording the deaths of large numbers of brothers and sisters. (There is a fine but horrifying example of this in the National Museum of Wales.) A sampler by Hannah Fieldhouse in the Guildford Museum records the initials of her parents and eight children. Two of the latter have died, and she simply puts 'is not' over the appropriate initials.

A sampler in the Victoria and Albert Museum shows a gentleman in a scarlet jacket labelled 'This is my dear father'. This speaks more truly of filial devotion than the often repeated sampler inscription 'by this you see, my parents took much care of me'.

One wonders how often the many cats and dogs which appear on samplers are portraits of pets. A boat, clearly named 'The Dora', on a sampler in the Norwich Museum Collection, must surely have had some personal significance.

Unfinished samplers also are intriguing. Was the work thrown aside and forgotten as the reluctant child grew up, or was it because

> "When Spring appears, when violets grow,
>   And shed a rich perfume,
>   How soon the fragrance breathes its last
>   How short-lived is the bloom?"

We shall never know, but samplers do stir romantic thoughts about their makers, and this is part of their charm.

A different kind of sampler typical of the eighteenth century was the

Right. A Hollie point sampler showing the exquisite fineness of the needle-made lace effect.
By courtesy of the Victoria and Albert Museum.

Hollie point sampler. Hollie point is a type of needle-made lace quite different in appearance from the elaborate cut and drawn work of the seventeenth century. The effect of the latter is of a strong white pattern standing boldly against a black ground, while the effect of the former is the reverse of this. A black pattern stands out against a white ground, but the pattern is delicate because the work is so fine (page 75). The illustration shows some completed work, and some material cut away for more work to begin. The method of work is very similar to detached buttonhole stitch (page 61) and the pattern of little black dots is made simply by missing stitches in the row. The popularity of Hollie point lace remained for many years after the other types had disappeared, because its lightness and delicacy made it suitable for use on baby clothes.

The Hollie point sampler and the darning sampler (page 95) are the two examples of work from this period which have a practical significance in the working life of the women of the day. The general run of samplers were at this time far removed from the fashion of embroidery current in the eighteenth and early nineteenth centuries.

It is as needlework pictures that samplers from this period afford most interest to needlewomen today. The lay-out, and the choice of subject matter, the inscriptions and the borders all need careful management in relation to each other for the finished work to be successful. In early samplers the patterns lie so close together that their full impact is not developed. Now there is a certain spaciousness in the lay-out of the finest samplers which suggests not only that material is not so prohibitively expensive as formerly, but also that the worker realised that space around motifs, and uncluttered background, had a value in themselves.

Everyone is familiar with the type of motif favoured by sampler workers. Rural scenes were very popular and trees came in every shape and size. Conical trees were ideal for working in cross stitch. Apple trees were a favourite, especially in conjunction with Adam and Eve, a biblical subject which retained its popularity. Houses and cottages are another favourite theme, usually complete with every detail of front steps, door knockers and garden gates. It is tempting to suppose that many of them were accurate representations of houses lived in by the children who worked them, but confidence in this theory is shattered by a sampler in the Victoria and Albert Museum which shows a nice, neat dwelling with five windows and two chimneys confidently labelled 'The Queen's Palace'. Houses also formed a favourite constituent of samplers in the United States, where a good deal of research has been done in attempting to identify them.

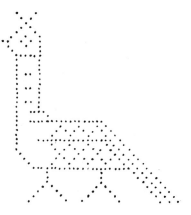

A Hollie point peacock

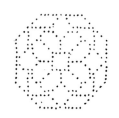

A Hollie point flower motif

A dovecote to work in block satin stitc

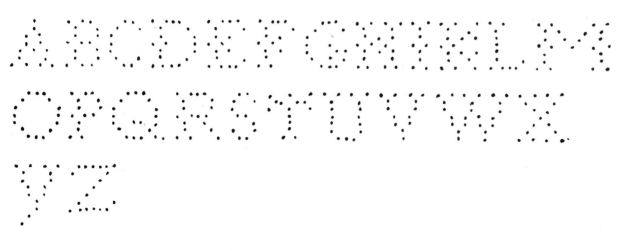

Dovecotes and windmills were popular motifs set in little rural scenes of trees and flowers. The familiar shape of the carnation was as popular at the end of the period of sampler making, as it was in the seventeenth century. In fact the recurrence of some of the most popular flower shapes can be a pit-fall to the unwary who wish to put a date on samplers. Urns and vases of every imaginable shape displayed floral arrangements, often a little stiffly.

Forts and ships were used occasionally, the latter with passengers amusingly placed, falling off tenders when the skill of worker proved inadequate to deal with the difficulties of the subjects.

A balanced lay-out was favoured by most workers, so that a house tended to have identical trees on each side, and a bird on the left would have another facing it on the right, and so on. It was only when this symmetry became too rigid that the design suffered and rural and garden scenes helped to break it up.

The real size of objects in relation to each other caused little trouble in the composition of sampler designs. Large birds could perch happily on small cottage chimneys and single flowers be placed near trees of similar size. This is a convention which causes no trouble to the observer, and is an essential part of the genre.

The best samplers of this later period show a happy combination of fancy and gaiety. One can imagine that they were good fun to work, and that the choice and placing of the motifs engaged the family of the worker in pleasant discussions. When finished they were framed and displayed as a proof of the child's skill, and as decorative objects in their own right. That they are still treasured by lucky descendants and eagerly sort after in antique shops shows how successful they were.

Above. Another border, in Hollie point
Below. A Hollie point alphabet

Sampler 7. Alphabets

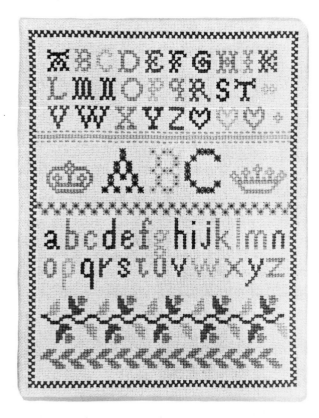

Alphabets and samplers are inextricably linked together in people's minds. The number of pieces worked which contained only alphabets must far out-number any other kind, and the reason for this is not hard to find. Their execution provided for the pupil a double lesson, the learning of letters and the learning of needlework. As the process of sewing was slow and painstaking, one may assume that the nimble-fingered pupil would know her alphabet even though she might be slow-witted, whilst the clumsy child would be even better grounded in the elements of learning by the time her work was completed.

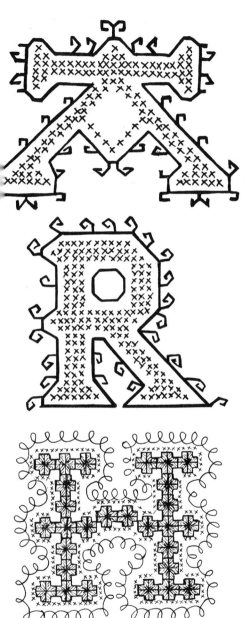

Initial letters for working in cross stitch, double running stitch or back stitch

Alphabets first began to appear in early seventeenth century samplers. A famous example is one by Ann Gower, an English girl who crossed the Atlantic for America in 1628. Her sampler, which has lettering worked in satin and eyelet stitches, can still be seen in the Essex Institute, Salem, USA. (Quoted by Miss Colby [*Samplers*, Batsford 1964] from Leigh Ashton, *Samplers*.)

By the eighteenth century alphabets were an expected constituent of samplers. Education for girls was becoming more widespread, and even the village dame could provide adequate instruction for sampler making. It was in fact an ideal medium, as it kept the child busy for long hours, and did not require a great reservoir of learning on the part of the instructor!

Charity foundations at one end of the social scale and private schools at the other also encouraged their production, though for different reasons. Skill in fine needlework was still an expected accomplishment of the well-bred girl, but charity schools had a more utilitarian approach. Their girls had to be equipped to earn their living either as maids of all types or as seamstresses. Samplers worked in schools must surely have been used as testimonials by girls seeking either private employment or apprenticeships.

The Charity School Movement began in the reign of Queen Anne with the avowed aim of 'teaching poor children the alphabet and the principles of religion'. Foundling Hospitals started in 1739, and the Orphan Working Home in 1758. The most famous of all alphabet samplers were those produced by the Bristol Orphanage during the nineteenth century (see page 80). They display an amazing number of scripts, Roman, Gothic and Italic, following one upon the other, with hardly a thread of unworked linen to be seen. Beneath is always a wide selection of narrow strip patterns, worked in red silk.

Samplers sometimes show elaborate initial letters, using a combination of stitches (see opposite) but on the whole lettering concentrated on a simplicity and legibility still pleasing to the twentieth century eye. Cross stitch was the most favoured stitch for this reason. Originally worked in all the reversible types (see page 22) cross stitch survived into the nineteenth century in its simpler form, along with four-sided stitch.

Algerian eye stitch was also a favourite because the hole pulled in the centre of each stitch helps to concentrate the eye on the essential shape of the letter. It is true to say that examples of lettering can be found worked in every embroidery technique used in samplers.

Alphabets were usually set out in strips across the sampler, divided by lines of pattern of varying complexity. Sometimes the letters were

Jesus, permit thy gracious name to stand,
As the first efforts of an infant's hand;
And, while her fingers on the canvass move,
Engage her tender thoughts to seek thy love,
With thy dear children let her have a part,
And write thy name thyself upon her heart.

M A Tipper
New Orphan House
North Wing
Ashley Down
Bristol
1808

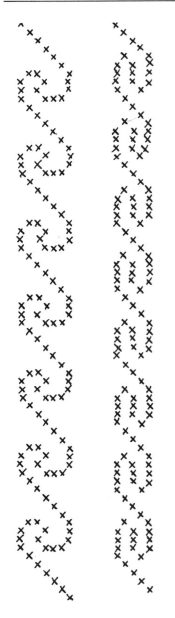

Above. Extra cross stitch borders

Left. An early nineteenth century
charity school sampler.
By courtesy of the Fitzwilliam Museum.

doubled (A.A, B.B, C.C), with two different stitches being employed. Sometimes they appeared as Aa, Bb, Cc, but usually the whole alphabet is given with capitals first and lower case letters set out below. The different types might follow directly one after the other, or alternatively any spaces might be filled up with space-fillers, such as spots, crosses or heart-shapes.

Many samplers of the eighteenth century still used the old alphabet, from which J and U were omitted, I and V doing duty for them when necessary. Z was sometimes left out as not being a letter in great demand. Q was written as the reverse of P, and does not take its modern form until the nineteenth century.

The main use that a housewife made of the skill learnt in working her alphabet sampler was in the marking and dating of household linen. (For numerals, see page 108.) It is a pity that this practice has been abandoned because many people own linen inherited from their mothers and grandmothers, about which it would be intriguing to know more.

The practice of embroidering crowns on samplers was originally part of the linen-marking process. Each rank of the nobility had its distinctive coronet, and the linen of great houses would be marked with the appropriate symbol above the initials of the owner, the date of acquisition and possibly the number of the article within a batch. In the Maritime Museum, Greenwich, there is some linen belonging to Lord Nelson, marked with his initials and coronets.

However, crowns are pretty, small and easy to work, and so useful for filling in an awkward space that this must surely be the main reason for their popularity as sampler patterns.

It is worthwhile for the modern embroiderer to learn to mark clearly and decoratively, because this practice can give considerable satisfaction to the worker on the completion of a piece, and it may also be of interest in the future. This interest may be confined to one's immediate family, but might have a wider, unforeseen interest for future generations. Chance still plays a great part in the survival or destruction of embroidery.

The alphabets and patterns which form this sampler come from the Victoria and Albert Museum. The first is mid-eighteenth century work, the second mid-nineteenth century. The crowns come from a group in a sampler to be seen in the Embroiderers' Guild Study Portfolio of Samplers.

The rectangular shape reflects the change which came over the size of samplers in the eighteenth century. They were made with a frame,

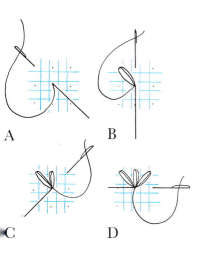

Algerian eye stitch

Left. Hearts and double hearts, crowns and borders in cross stitch, useful as fillers in alphabet samplers

either simple or elaborate, and were intended to be displayed to show off a child's skill.

This is a very easy sampler to work.

Count of cotton: 16 threads to the inch.

Size of design: Border encloses an area of $13\frac{1}{2} \times 10\frac{1}{2}$ in.

> A. $9\frac{1}{2} \times 3$ in.
> B. $9\frac{1}{2} \times 3$ in.
> C. $9\frac{1}{2} \times 3$ in.
> D. $9\frac{1}{2} \times 3$ in.

Thread: Anchor Soft Embroidery.

Overall size of material: 18×14 in.

Size of finished work: 15×12 in.

To adapt the design to other types of fabric, see Chapter II, Scale, cross stitch.

To prepare the material, see Chapter II, Method of Work.

Allow $2\frac{1}{2}$ in. at the top of the work. Begin by working the top and the sides of the border, in alternating cross stitch (page 21). There will be 45 cross stitches in the top row, 44 below. Start from the central tacking thread and work outwards. Work down the sides for about 13 in., but do not finish the bottom rows. This will give you a little leeway in the spacing of the alphabets and patterns, and should be finished when the rest of the work is completed.

Follow the charts for the positioning of the alphabets. Work in cross, Algerian eye, and running stitch.

To make up, see Chapter VII.

Algerian eye stitch

This stitch is worked over a square of four threads each way. Use a tapestry needle.

Come up in the centre, and make a stitch diagonally over two threads into the corner of the square. Come up the centre again, and repeat the stitch.

Now work round the square, always coming up in the middle and always keeping two threads between the stitches on the edge of the square. In this way you will work round, making little spokes. On completing the stitch you will have worked eight spokes, sixteen stitches in all. The spokes will be alternately diagonal and straight. When completed there will be a clear central hole. This stitch looks well worked in a light colour, which will show up the dark hole.

Overleaf. Patterns for sampler 7

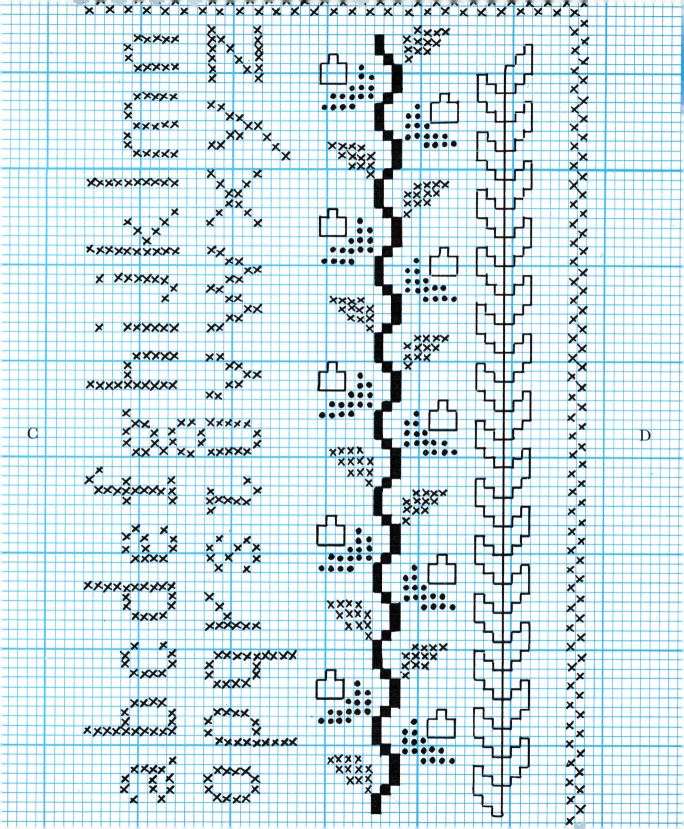

C   D

Sampler 8. Spring

There are some problems to be considered in the best use of inscriptions in embroidery, and these were not solved quickly by the makers of samplers.

The early inscriptions are often very difficult to read, not because the letters were badly proportioned, but because the lay-out was confused. Capitals and lower case letters of the same size were often mixed indiscriminately with quaint results. For instance in 1713 we find Elizabeth Harris writing Lead US NOT INtO TEMPtation bUt deLIUer US from eUIL, and incidently using U's when her contemporaries used V's.

There was generally a lack of spacing between words, and between inscriptions, names and dates. Lines of poems might be split up with bands of patterns between them, but the whole was so tightly put together that the total effect was one of pattern, not of writing intended to be read.

By the end of the eighteenth century the problems of lay-out had been solved and there are many samplers with beautifully proportioned clear inscriptions, even when the writing is minuscule.

Clarity depends on there being a distinct difference in size between capitals and lower case letters, though tall letters may be as high as the capitals. Assuming the stitch to be cross stitch worked over two threads, each letter needs two threads between it and the following one. Words need a six thread separation. These proportions will keep the letters grouped into word units, and the words grouped into sentence units to ensure easy reading. Lines must also be carefully spaced so that there is a two thread separation between the tails of g's and y's on one line and any high letters on the row beneath. Failure to allow for this can lead to a very awkward situation. Too big a space between lines can be a fault, as the lines do not seem to belong together.

The choice of an inscription is a difficult task. Original inscriptions may be amusing but they are not usually to our taste. Verses from favourite poems are often unmanageable because of their length and because we are not prepared to work on such a tiny scale as our ancestors. One can sympathise with workers who look no further than 'Bless this house' or 'Home, Sweet Home'. The poem on the sampler is by William Blake and its lyrical quality suits the typical motifs of birds, trees and flowers. It has the merit of having very short lines, except for the last, and the lines themselves create quite a pleasant pattern. From the working sketch you will see that each line has been aligned to the central thread. This is not necessary for every sort of poem, but it should always be done for the title and the first line. Succeeding lines may fall into place below the first.

The easiest and fool-proof way to do this (and it is very easy to make mistakes in calculating the space needed for lettering), is to work it out carefully using two sheets of graph paper. On one draw a central line down the sheet. On the other sketch out your title, having chosen your lettering and capitals. Cut out this slip of paper, fold it carefully in half, and pin it to the first sheet with the fold mark on the central line.

Now sketch out your first line, cut and fold it, and pin it below the title, fold to line as before.

Prepare the second line, cut, but do not fold it in two. You can now get an idea of how your inscription will look. Adjust the spaces between

SPRING

Sound the flute!
Now it's mute.
Birds delight
Day and night:
Nightingale
In the dale:
Lark in sky
Merrily
Merrily merrily to welcome in the year.

Layout for sampler 8

the lines until you are satisfied that they are the right distance apart. Allow space for your capitals and space below the line for your tailed letters.

Experiment with the second line and see if it looks better either centred or starting directly below the first line. When you are satisfied, stick your loose pieces of paper carefully in position.

It would be a safeguard to work out any other lines in the same way, though you might not find this essential. Remember that in your calculations extra space is needed to separate one verse from another.

Pattern for sampler 8

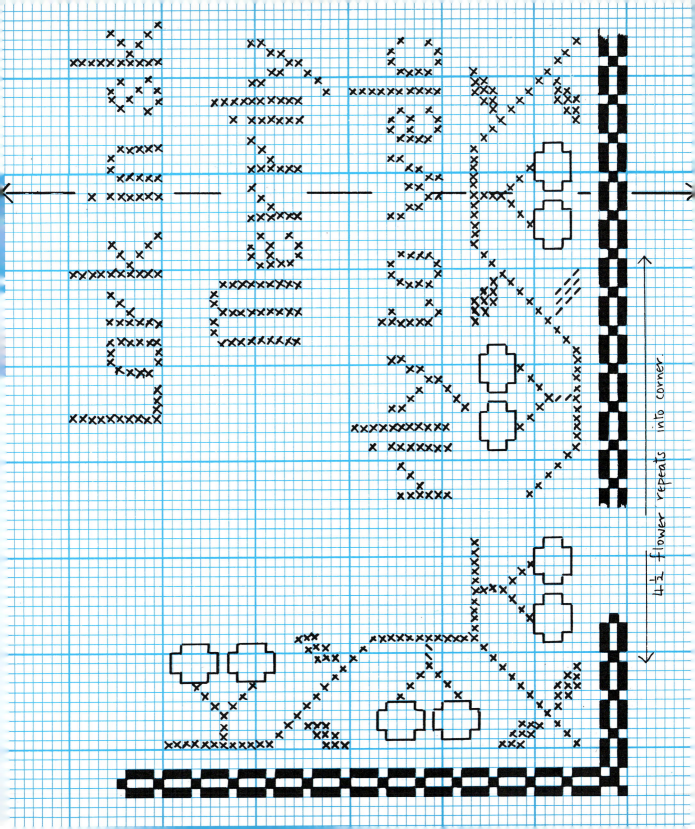

4½ flower repeats into corner.

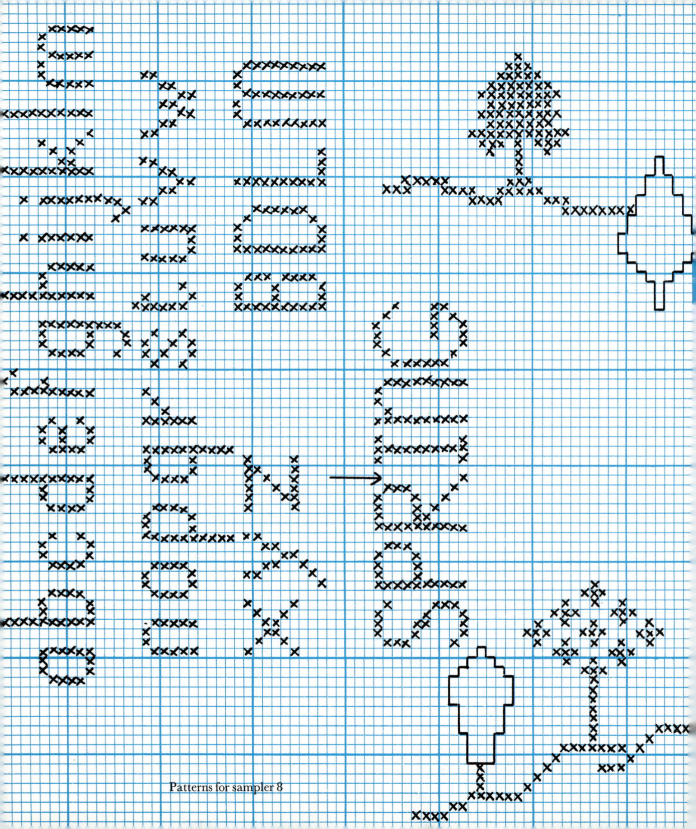

Patterns for sampler 8

B

B.

C

This process may seem long and tedious, but in fact it can be done quite quickly. Though the letters and spacing must be accurately counted, the drawing can be quite rough. In the end you will have a pattern which will give you correct results.

For working, start from the central point and work outwards for any lines which have been aligned to the central thread. Lines that lie directly below the one above can be worked from the line beginning.

It is sensible to draft out your inscription before you make any decisions as to what motifs or what border to use. Lettering cannot be squeezed in. Motifs can be chosen to fit the spaces left, and borders can be adapted to different sizes (see Sampler 10).

The lettering in this sampler is a simplified and modernised form of that used in the Alphabet Sampler. The borders and the motifs all come from the National Museum of Wales (St Fagan's) and were worked by Mary Grinnes, Mary Ann Heydon, Elizabeth Gwyther and others in the early years of the nineteenth century. The pyramid trees are common to many samplers.

Count of linen: 21 threads to the inch.

Size of main designs: Borders 20 in. square
$1\frac{1}{2}$ in. wide.

Inscription 14 in. long × 16 in. at the widest point.

Trees A. $2\frac{1}{4}$ in. long
B. $4\frac{1}{2}$ in. long
C. $3\frac{3}{4}$ in. long.

Thread: DMC Coton Perlé No. 8.

Overall size of material: 27 in. square.

Size of finished sampler: 22 in. square.

To adapt to other fabrics, see Chapter II under Scale, cross stitch.

To prepare the material, see Chapter II, Method of Work.

Begin by working the border, starting with the central thread aligned to the centre of the border marked on the chart. Allow three inches from the bottom of your material, starting on the base line of the pattern.

Now work the lettering. It will be easier to place it correctly if you start at the bottom. Count six threads up, to start with the bottom of the W of welcome.

The central pyramid tree A should be on the centre line, with the others spaced evenly on either side, an inch apart. For the spacing of the other trees, flowers and birds there is no necessity to get a perfect balance by the counted thread.

For finishing, see Chapter VII.

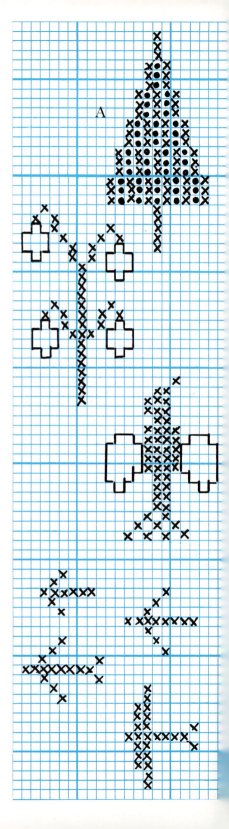

Sampler 9. Darning

Just at the time when samplers were becoming more stereotyped in their arrangement and showing far less technical excellence than formerly, a new and interesting phenomenon occurred – the darning samplers. These date from the closing decades of the eighteenth century, into the early years of the nineteenth.

In the late eighteenth century, the sampler, for all its undoubted charm, was not a true reflection either of the needs of the practical

Left. Patterns for sampler 8

working needlewoman of the time, or of the embroidery fashions of the day. Now the sampler once more took a practical turn.

The darning sampler was basically an exercise in darning. Some which survive have such horrid slashes deliberately made in the material that, even with two centuries intervening, one shudders for the poor child confronted with the mending of them. These slashes were carefully darned together, the thread following the weave of the material. Sometimes a matching thread was used, but more often a contrasting one.

Square holes were also cut in the fabric, and the hole carefully repaired in threads of two colours, worked first across and then down the hole, making a decorative cross on the fabric. Sometimes these holes were filled with simulated knitting, worked in silk.

The patterns of these darns are a most interesting study. They range from the simplest tabby weave (under and over alternate threads) through every variety of twill and herringbone, to the most complex damask patterns. Mastering these skills as a child, the housewife would be able to tackle mending fine hosiery, damask table linen, and the delicate muslin used for garments at this period, which by its very fragility must often have needed attention.

That the fashion for making darning samplers was spread across the whole social spectrum can be judged from the materials used in making them. The most homely were worked on very coarse fabrics, which looked like, and probably were, flour or sugar bags salvaged by thrifty mothers when their primary function was fulfilled.

The most beautiful of these samplers were worked on very delicate fabrics. This is variously described as tiffany, or isabelline gauze, a name which describes the colour as well as the texture of the material. The Isabel in question was a lady of the seventeenth century who rashly vowed not to change her linen until her husband took the town of Ostend which he was beseiging for the Spanish. Unfortunately the operation took longer than she had expected, and at the end of three years her linen had taken on a dull yellow hue! In fact the fabric is quite attractive.

Tiffany was a delicate silk gauze described by an angry moralist as 'instead of apparel to cover and hide, shews women naked'. This period was the age of the 'naked fashion' when women abandoned most of their underpinning and petticoats and went abroad wearing the finest silks, gauzes and muslins. It is fascinating to observe that such a fundamental upheaval as the French Revolution, which inspired these free (and often scandalous) fashions, should have repercussions on the small domestic world of sampler making. Nobody would buy

Right. Late eighteenth century darning sampler with a flower garland in the centre.
By courtesy of the Victoria and Albert Museum.

95

expensive material specifically, so these samplers must have been made from off-cuts of fashion garments.

The best of these darning samplers have a delicate fragility and charm which is quite enchanting. The ugly slashes made in the coarser work are not to be seen here, though the square crosses of darning remain. The centre of the work is often taken up with a delicate bouquet of mixed flowers, tied with ribbon, and with stray leaves and flowers scattered around. The outlines of the flowers are worked in stem stitch, and the fillings are darned in twill patterns in coloured silks. (See page 95.)

The making of these amazingly delicate patterns needed very fine needles, and once again sampler-making reflects the wider movements of history. Towards the end of the eighteenth century developments in steel making, stimulated by the industrial revolution, made the production of very fine needles possible. Without this development, the sewing of this type of work would have been impossible.

Patterned darning has interesting possibilities in modern embroidery. It works in well with modern blackwork, and when worked on a bold scale has a certain 'ethnic' quality which is appealing to the modern eye. It is also interesting to work with because of the way the darning process mutes the colours used.

The sampler given here is a simple arrangement of leaf-shapes, suggested by some of the floral darning samplers. It is easy to work, as long as the first row in each pattern is carefully counted. The patterns are common to most darning samplers, so no numbers are given for references to museum collections.

Count of linen: 33 threads to the inch.

Diameter of ring: $11\frac{1}{2}$ in.

Central diamonds: 5×5 in.

Thread: Danish Flower Threads.

Overall size of fabric needed: 18 in. square or 20 in. according to the finish.

Finished size: 16 in square.

No calculations need be made to make this sampler on a different count of fabric, because the darning patterns will fill in shapes of any size and any count of thread. Also the basic leaf shape given is so simple that it can be drawn to any size to suit the worker.

Prepare the linen, marking both the vertical and horizontal central threads with a tacking thread.

To mark the circular pattern of leaves on the fabric without the use of a pair of compasses:

1. Draw the circumference of a large dinner plate on to a piece of

Two carnations, one in block satin stitch and the other in darning stitch

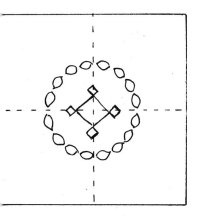

Layout for sampler 9

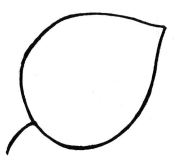

Shape for leaf pattern

domestic greaseproof paper.

2. Fold the paper in half, matching the pencil line carefully. Make a sharp edge on the fold with your fingernail.

3. Repeat the folding process three times, making sharp edges on each fold.

4. Open up your paper, which should now have sixteen perfectly spaced lines, radiating from the centre, to the edge of the circle.

The leaves may now be drawn or traced in position, one filling up the space on the circumference, between each fold line.

Pin the paper to your fabric, making sure that your horizontal and vertical tacking lines match with corresponding fold lines in the paper pattern. Pin the centres of paper and fabric together carefully, to make sure that it is accurately placed.

Tack round each leaf shape with little stitches, and then carefully tear away the paper.

Your sampler is now ready to work.

Eight simple darning patterns are given (pages 98-99) each to be worked twice, opposite each other.

Use strong colours as they will be toned down in the darning process.

Surround the leaves with stem stitch (page 53) giving each leaf a short stem.

Leave the central diamonds to the end, when you will be familiar with working twill patterns.

Start where the two tacking lines intersect and leave about four inches of thread hanging loose behind the work.

Bring the needle up on one side of the central thread, go down over it, under three, over one, to the end of the row (fourteen stitches on the chart).

Now thread your needle with the short end and work in the opposite direction (thirteen stitches).

You now have a balanced row, with thirteen stitches on both sides, and one in the middle of your line.

With the long thread again in your needle, begin to work the twill pattern. As you approach the central stitch, take up five threads instead of three then continue as before. This will change the direction of the twill. As you work from side to side the diamond shape will be established. The second time you come to the centre, take up three threads, the next time one thread, the next time five threads, and so on.

If you follow the chart carefully for the first few lines the pattern will soon become so clearly established that the stitching is very easy, and you will not need the chart at all.

When the work comes to a point, weave the thread in at the back.

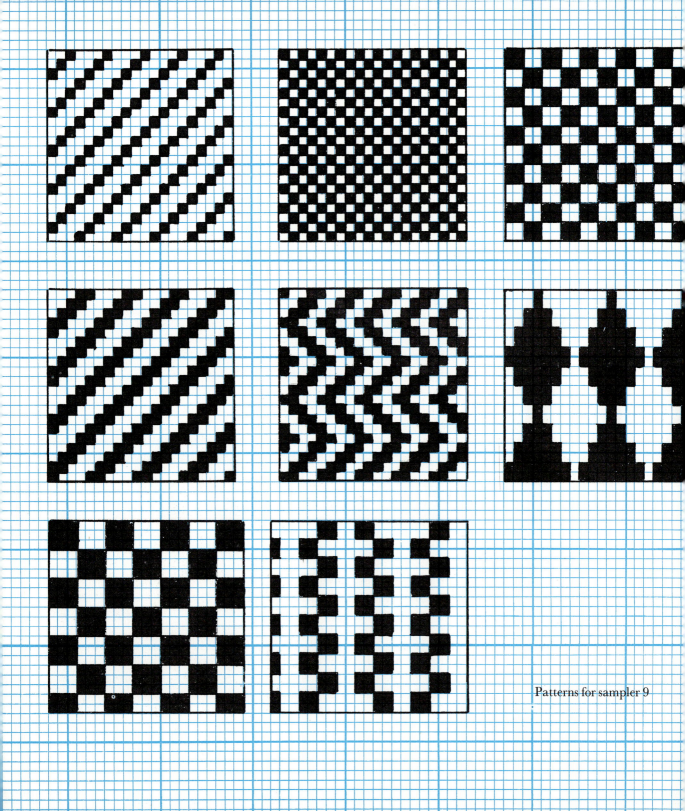

Patterns for sampler 9

Start again and work the other side of the diamond.

The small diamonds are worked one from each point of the large one. Start by counting out the central line of the pattern. Work one side, and then the other. These are a little more difficult and the chart must be followed carefully for each line of stitching.

To make up, see Chapter VII.

Patterned darning

This is simply a counted running stitch, and by varying the threads picked up by the needle all sorts of patterns can be made.

The first rows need careful counting, but soon the pattern is established and it is easy to do.

In the diagrams the black squares represent the coloured thread you are working with, and the plain squares are the threads you pick up. Work to and fro across the area you wish to fill, with a row of stitching between each fabric thread.

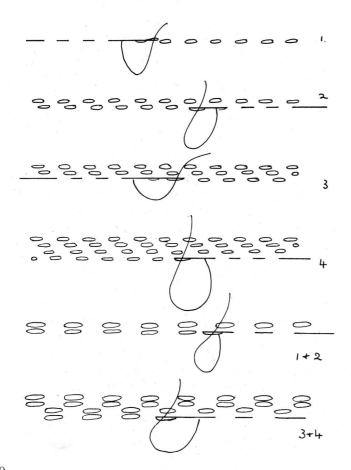

Patterned darning stitch

Sampler 10. Home and Abroad

Borders are an essential part of later samplers, and their correct management presents some problems. The study of samplers shows that the working of borders and corners often caused the most awkward dilemmas. Some corners are very peculiar indeed, while others are managed with great expertise.

The working of corners from geometrical band patterns is not of course confined to sampler making, and it is a skill worth mastering for its many practical uses. The most sophisticated way of working this out is by the use of a mirror. A handbag mirror or a mirror tile is the best

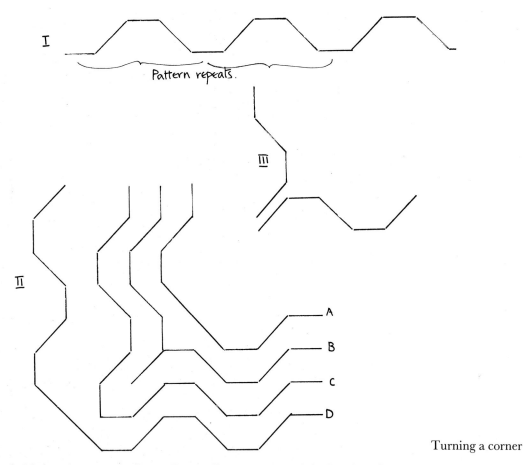

I

Pattern repeats.

III

II

A

B

C

D

Turning a corner

tool. If you place your mirror diagonally across a straight border, the diagonal line it makes becomes the mitre of your corner. The full corner can be seen by looking at the pattern and into the mirror at the same time. By moving the mirror along the pattern different corners form themselves, and you can choose the one that you like the best. It can then be sketched on graph paper.

Floral borders are not treated in this way, but the patterns are nevertheless adaptable to various lengths to suit the needs of the design. The method for calculating the length of the border you need, and how to make a corner from it, will be easier to understand by studying the diagrams above.

Figure I shows the basic shape of a border and the length of its pattern repeats. When you know the number of stitches in your pattern repeat you can calculate its length in inches on your chosen fabric, and

Let gratitude in acts of goodness flow
Our love to God in love to man below
Be this our joy to calm the troubled breast
Support the weak and succour the distrest
Direct the wandrer dry the widows tear
The orphan guard the sinking spirits cheer
Though small our power to act though mean our skill
God sees the heart he judges by the will

Mary Pether 1839

Nineteenth century domestic scene.
The border pattern is a particularly
pretty one, given on page 110.
*By courtesy of the Victoria and Albert
Museum.*

also how many repeats will be needed to make up the length you require. You must have an odd number of repeats in your line, because you must start at the central tacking thread in the middle of a pattern.

Figure II shows the basic pattern with the corner turned at three different points. A and D are the same, but D is one pattern repeat longer. B makes a border five stitches longer than A, and C makes a border five stitches longer than B. From this information you can choose the corner which suits your calculations best. Study of the borders of Samplers 8 and 10 will show two differently made corners.

Some samplers use two different borders, one up the sides and another along the top and bottom. Figure III shows how these can be placed to make a neat corner.

When preparing fabric for work which includes a border not only must the central vertical thread be marked with a tacking, but the central horizontal thread also. This is essential for placing the design.

A sampler with a square border is the easiest to manage because one set of calculations will take you round the square. However, it is not too difficult to lengthen the sides in units of the pattern repeat. By measuring up half the length of your side, from the central horizontal thread, you will find the correct position to start working the top section of the border from the vertical central thread.

A rough sketch, preferably on graph paper, will help you to visualise your calculations. It is also wise for a beginner to allow a reasonable margin of fabric, because it is always possible to make a mistake.

The sampler 'Home and Abroad' is worked in cross stitch, with some four-sided stitch. The ship was originally worked by Esther Haines in 1822 and the house by A.S. in 1819.

Aida thread count: 12 blocks to the inch.

Size of main designs: A. Border 16 × 14 in.

                       B. House 5 × 5 in.

                       E. Ship 7 × 6 in.

Thread: Danish Mat Garn.

Overall size of material needed: 20 in × 18 in.

Size of finished sampler: 17 in. × 14½ in.

To adapt to other fabrics, see Chapter II, under Scale, cross stitch.

To prepare the material, see Chapter II, Method of Work.

Allow three inches at the top of the fabric, and work the border, starting from the central tacking thread. Now work the house B. Count eighteen threads down from the border by the central tacking thread, and start with the roof.

When you have worked the house, you will find that the charts for the other motifs link together and the motifs are easy to position.

To finish, see Chapter VII.

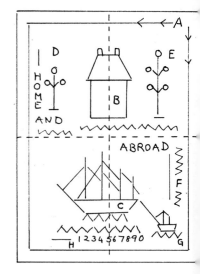

Layout for sampler 10

Right, and following pages. Patterns for sampler 10. Note that the letters indicate where the patterns fit together

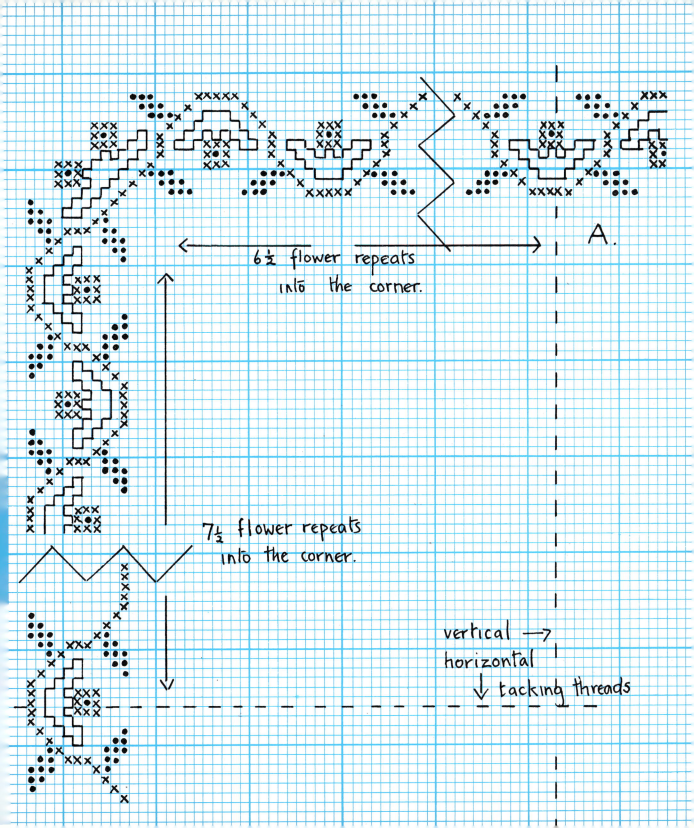

6½ flower repeats into the corner.

7½ flower repeats into the corner.

A.

vertical →
horizontal
↓ tacking threads

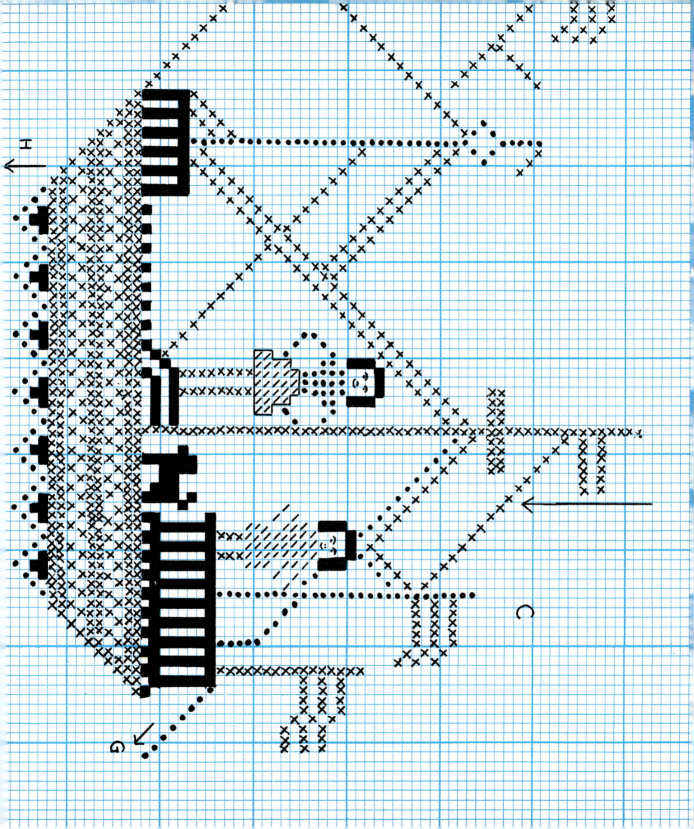

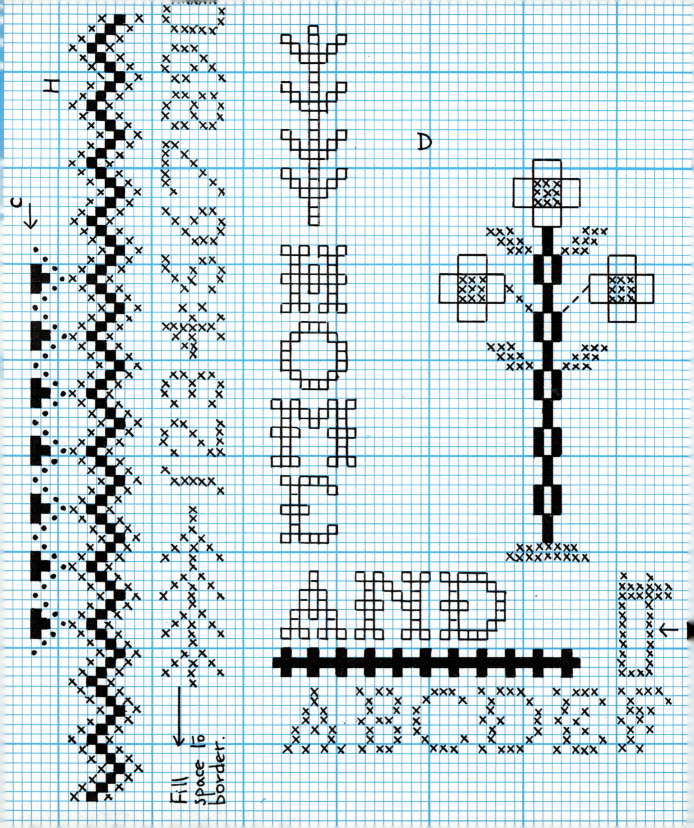

H

c

D

Fill
space to
border.

AND

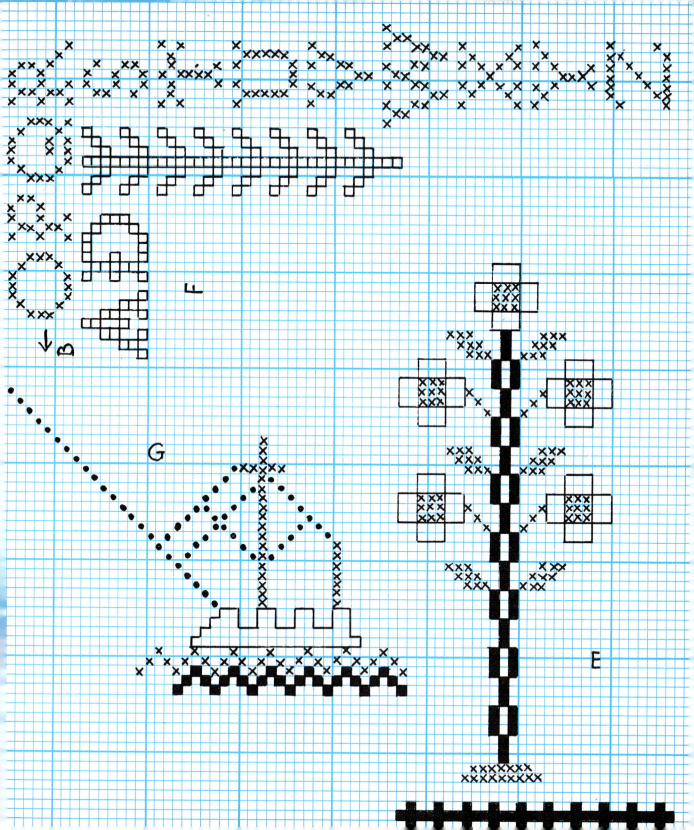

VI
DECLINE AND
REVIVAL

For three hundred years the sampler had played a dominant part in the development of amateur or domestic needlework skills, but by the middle of the nineteenth century various factors combined to end its long reign.

In the first place the form itself began to suffer from too much repetition. So many thousands of samplers had been made that inevitably imitation led to a loss of vitality, and designs became more meagre and more stereotyped. The demand for sampler-making material created a market for commercially drawn linen which put an end to the delightful spontaneity and freshness of original work. Printed outlines for map samplers, available in the eighteenth century, are an example of the best of these. The outlines were likely to have more semblance to reality than if they had been drawn by a teacher or a pupil, but commercially drawn patterns could only have a deadening effect, especially when the stitch was confined to cross stitch.

At the beginning of the nineteenth century a new fashion in canvas work developed in Germany, and soon spread to England. This was Berlin wool work. Worked in strong colours on double or Penelope canvas, it consisted originally of a variety of stitches, but these almost immediately declined to tent stitch and cross stitch. The designs, worked out on graph paper, and coloured with realistic shading, were either floral or pictorial.

Wools, canvas and charts were imported into England in great quantities, but soon we were producing our own materials to satisfy what can only be described as a craze. By mid-century middle class drawing room walls were adorned by wool work pictures with such subjects as Rebecca at the Well, or the Infant Prince of Wales. Fire screens and cushions had designs of waxy lilies and lush, overblown

Left. Some extra cross stitch borders

roses, while papa relaxed wearing slippers embroidered with three-dimensional pansies.

At first a few Berlin work samplers were produced, and the elaborate shading which this type of work favoured was introduced into the old sampler patterns, but soon this new fashion helped to speed the end of the sampler by the availability of charts and written instructions.

From the end of the eighteenth century magazines for women were being published, and soon they became a flood to satisfy the demands of the growing middle class. *The Englishwoman's Domestic Magazine, The Work-Table Magazine, Woman as Virgin, Wife and Mother, Fancywork* and *Embroidery* are but a few of the publications which were available. The *Work-Table Magazine* had the same format as the German pattern leaflets. About the size of small diaries or postcards, they consisted of a concertina-like pull-out of charts. On one side there were alphabets, numerals and geometric patterns, on the other side pictures of animals, fruit and flowers, all elaborately shaded and printed on graph paper.

One publication specifically designed for children was *The Embroidery and Alphabet Sampler Book*. Designed to fit into a child's small pocket or work bag, it had a bright green cover and a pull-out of thirty-two tiny pages, eight each printed in mauve, green, red and blue. It consisted of flower-wreathed designs of girl's names, such as Rose, Emily and Ellen, several sets of alphabets and numerals, crowns, orbs and sceptres, geometric patterns, farm animals and such domestic paraphernalia as top-hats and birdcages. No doubt some of these designs found their way into samplers, but it is clear that with all these fascinating patterns to hand the Victorian child did not need to work a sampler. She could select the designs she wished to work on her needlecase, her purse, the bell-pull for mamma, or the slippers for papa.

Victorian children were also finding new types of handwork for their busy fingers. Knitting on the whole was a humdrum domestic activity, producing stockings and vests, but crochet, tatting and netting were more exciting. Lace collars, caps, antimacassars and doyleys were much more exciting to make than the old-fashioned samplers, and leaflets and pattern books were easily obtainable.

The amazing vitality and real practical value of the sampler as a medium for instruction was not yet spent, however. The first domestic sewing machines were invented by the middle of the century, and one was exhibited at the Great Exhibition in 1851. This wonderful invention, though welcomed whole-heartedly into the domestic scene, took a long time to alter the attitude of mothers and teachers to the teaching of plain sewing.

Nineteenth century alphabet and other motifs, from contemporary pattern books

Professional dress and shirt makers may have supplied the rich with their personal linen, but most households in the nineteenth century expected to make their own. The availability of cheap calico, with its wonderful wearing and washing qualities, had improved the standard of underwear, but big families were the rule and clothing them was a considerable task. Instruction in plain sewing at this time was of a very high standard, and the chosen medium was the sampler.

Plain sewing samplers are often quite tiny, perhaps only six inches long, by four inches wide, but on these tiny pieces of calico are recorded a vast number of techniques. Running, hemming, seaming of various types, tucking, gathering, setting in gussets, attaching pockets, making buttons and buttonholes and sewing on tapes are only a few of the more obvious ones.

The Norwich Museum (Stranger's Hall) has a very fine collection, including a book of samplers produced by the Female Model School, Dublin, in the middle of the century. It starts off with instructions for hemming and the sampler is made of green paper. It was not until this task was accomplished with reasonable skill that the child was given a small piece of calico. The seventh sampler in this carefully graded series of lessons is a most beautifully made shirt. It is complete with a yoke, a pleated front, sleeves set in with under-arm gussets, cuffs set on to beautifully stroked gathers, and a neck-bank with buttonholes neatly made. The whole garment, sewn in minuscule stitches, is just seven inches long. The same book includes a tiny frock with a delightful inset in the bodice worked with embroidery and drawn thread work.

The speed and efficiency of the sewing machine was to win in the end. The capacity of the domestic machine to do the basic sewing on a garment was quickly recognised, but this still left all the finer parts to be hand sewn. Commercial machines developed very quickly however, so that by the end of the Victorian era cheap clothes of all types were being produced on such a scale that the hand-making of underwear, shirts and blouses was no longer necessary. These could even be given decorative finishes because inventions for machine embroidery had kept pace with those for ordinary sewing.

However fond one may be of needlework, it must be recognised that these developments meant a release from what must have been a grinding servitude for many women. It is not surprising that at this point theories about the education of girls began to change radically. There were of course a large number of factors which made for women's emancipation, but these developments relieved women of their age-old role as garment-makers, and provided a new environment in which other changes could flourish.

Unfortunately the education that superceded the old system was so male-orientated that domestic skills were abandoned as an unnecessary subject for educated women, and in the present century several generations of girls have had virtually no education in needlework – a situation which many are now regretting.

Ironically, within a hundred years of the decay of the sampler an environment has been created in which the making of samplers could flourish again. The glorious machine age so eagerly welcomed by our forefathers has not fulfilled our expectations, and people generally feel a need to find satisfaction by some form of creative activity. Now that women have been relieved of the drudgery of endless handsewing, individuals can once again find satisfaction in embroidery. It is the lack of technical equipment to do this well which makes sampler making a practical exercise for the last decades of the twentieth century.

This fact has been recognised by a few individuals like the great Miss Louisa Pesel, who worked the stitch samplers for the Victoria and Albert Museum, and such specialist bodies as the National Federation of Women's Institutes who have encouraged the working of samplers for their specialist embroidery examinations, and the Embroiderers' Guild, who have an interesting collection of modern samplers.

Every embroiderer hopes to do inspirational work, but can be frustrated by a lack of technique. A good technical knowledge can speed the work, and help to keep the inspiration fresh. Samplers are not an end in themselves, but a step on the way to greater things. They provide the exercise by which an embroiderer learns her craft. They can be interesting to study, fun to work, and very decorative. They can in fact be beautiful. But above all they should have a practical relevance to the individual needs of the needlewomen who make them. This is how they began in the fifteenth and sixteenth centuries and how they need to be revived in the twentieth.

VII
FINISHING

Two types of finishing are suggested, to fit with the historical methods.

Early samplers were designed to be rolled on but not attached to a bar of wood or ivory. A modern adaptation of this method would be to hemstitch round the work, and at the top make a series of buttonhole loops, through which a piece of dowel could be threaded. The work can then be hung from this bar, as a wall panel.

Conventional samplers were framed as pictures, and the later samplers in the book would look better framed. More material is needed for mounting, and in all the sampler directions allowance has been made for this method. It is important to decide how you intend to finish the work before you actually begin.

Method 1. Hemstitching

Remove all tacking threads. Trim back the linen to a neat edge if necessary.

The hem should be as narrow as it is conveniently possible to make, depending on the weight of linen used. A wide hem makes the work look like a tray cloth.

For $\frac{1}{4}$ in. hem withdraw one thread from the linen, $\frac{3}{4}$ in. from the edge. Fold over twice, to make the hem just above the drawn thread line.

Follow the diagram for hemstitching, using a thread to match the linen. Run the thread into the hem, and work from left to right. Take up three threads from the drawn line, the needle pointing to the left.

Pull the needle through, and then with the needle pointing upwards, make a small stitch into the turned hem, and the back of the hem together. Pull the thread firmly. By these two actions the drawn threads are tied into bundles, and the hem secured.

Do not try to mitre the corner on such a narrow hem. Turn it as neatly as possible, snipping off a tiny corner of excess linen. Use a fine needle and cotton to neaten the outside of the corner with tiny stitches.

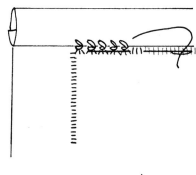
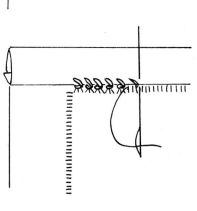

Hemstitching

Alternatives to Hemstitching

1. Materials such as Aida cannot be hemstitched, but a running stitched edge worked under and over the blocks in a thread to match the embroidery is very simple and looks well.

It is difficult to make a neat narrow hem in this material because of the weave, and a reasonable turning should always be allowed. Do your running stitch $1\frac{1}{2}$ in. from the edge. Then with a matching fine sewing cotton make a hem at the back $\frac{1}{2}$ in. wide.

2. Darning edge (Suitable for blackwork). Do three rows of patterned darning round the work. (See page 100.) A simple twill edge is effective. Then finish as above with a neat hem, invisibly sewn behind to the edge of the rows of darning.

To make the loops, see buttonhole bars (page 60).

Buy your dowelling rod first and cut it exactly to the width of your finished work. Sandpaper the ends. Gauge the size of your loops exactly to fit the rod.

Press your work carefully when all the sewing has been completed. Use a damp cloth, and press from the back. Be careful not to overpress.

Thread the dowelling through the loops and attach a fine cord for hanging your work.

Mounting a sampler as a picture

This can be done professionally, but it is not difficult to do yourself. An old picture frame may be of use, but art shops sell framing which they will mitre to the required size, leaving you to do the glueing. Prepare your frame before mounting the sampler. In this way you will get a better fit for the mount.

Cut a piece of hardboard to fit the recess in the frame. Use a set square if possible, and make the measurements $\frac{1}{8}-\frac{1}{4}$ in. smaller each way than the recess, to allow for the thickness of the material.

The hardboard should now be covered with material to give it a little padding. This is to prevent the embroidery and fabric from looking thin and strained. Bump is the ideal fabric, but a piece of wincyette or brushed cotton will do.

Lay the lining on a flat surface. Place the hardboard in the centre, and fold over one edge. Secure this with adhesive tape. Now do the opposite side, pulling it gently so that there are no wrinkles on the front. Secure this side with tape.

Trim the excess fabric from the corners, and repeat for the other two sides. (See figure.)

Now press your sampler carefully, having removed all tacking threads. Use a damp cloth, and press lightly from the back.

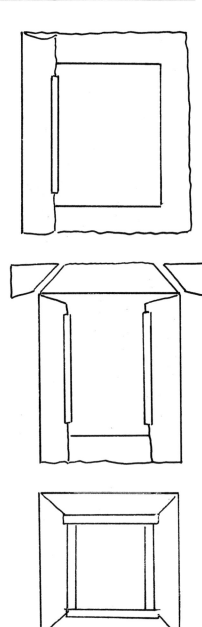

Lining the hardboard before mounting a sampler

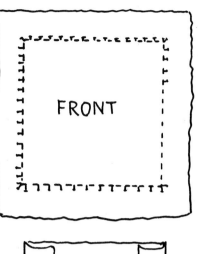

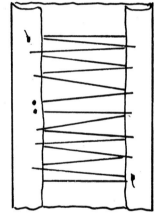

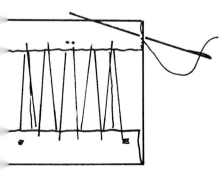

Lay the sampler over the padded front of the board, centring it carefully. Pin in position, putting the pins into the lining at right angles to the edge. Work along the top first, then along the bottom. Now pin the sides. In this way you can see clearly the positioning of your work. (See figure.) It *must* be meticulously straight.

When you are satisfied, turn the sampler face downwards. With a strong thread brace the material across the back of the hardboard. Start in the centre and work out to the corners in each case. (See figure.) Do not trim off the excess linen but fold it neatly and secure it with slip stitches.

End off your bracing threads securely.

The embroidery should now fit into the frame. It may need a sprig or two to hold it firmly in position.

If you have glass in your frame, the sampler will stay fresh for a long time. If it is unglazed you will have more pleasure in looking at it. If it is made of linen, when it is dirty, it can be taken from the frame, the bracing threads cut, and the work laundered. It is a simple matter to brace it again on its mount.

Mounting and lacing the sampler on the hardboard

VIII
STUDYING SAMPLERS

Visiting museums to study one's own particular interest can prove disappointing. Many museums with a good collection of samplers do not always display them for a variety of reasons.

Firstly, textiles will quickly deteriorate if placed perpetually in a good light. It is in the interests of preservation to keep them in a dimly lit corner, or better still, in the reserve collection.

The fashion for folk museums means that a few samplers are chosen for display within their historical contexts. Thus a strip sampler might be shown in a seventeenth century room beside a stumpwork box, or a nineteenth century one be hanging on the wall of a Victorian drawing room. This system has a great deal to commend it, but it does not provide much for the student with a specialised interest.

Problems of display generally, and the sheer bulk of museums' reserve collections (often as much as 99 per cent of the whole) does cause problems. Some museums do not attempt to display samplers except in occasional specially mounted exhibitions. Other museums lack a textile enthusiast in their applied arts departments and so valuable collections are a little neglected.

The Victoria and Albert Museum, which is avowedly educational in its constitution, provides an excellent study room for embroidery, with a good selection of samplers. Samplers are mounted behind glass in pull-out frames, and the student can study them under good conditions.

The Embroiderers' Guild provides for its members the excellent service of Study Portfolios, which members may borrow for limited periods and study in their own homes. This is a service of inestimable value, as the samplers can be handled and both sides of the work examined. There are two portfolios, an historical and a modern one. The Embroiderers' Guild also have a travelling exhibition, which can sometimes be seen at the Guild's Headquarters by appointment.

Anyone can become a member of the Guild by payment of the current subscription.

Museums vary very much in their attitudes towards the accessibility of their reserve collections. It must be remembered that availability of staff and security problems play a great part in forming these attitudes. It is up to the individual student to ask for permission to view collections, and to allow plenty of time for an appointment to be made.

This list of museums in the United Kingdom worth a visit does not pretend to be comprehensive.

Blaise Castle House Museum, Bristol. A few samplers on view.
The Fitzwilliam Museum, Cambridge. An excellent collection, not readily accessible. Available to bona fide scholars by appointment.
The National Museum of Wales (St Fagan's), Cardiff. A collection of middle and later periods, not readily accessible. Available to scholars by appointment.
The Dorset County Museum, Dorchester. A small selection on view. Reserved collection may be seen by appointment.
The Guildford Museum. A small but interesting permanent display, from early down to modern times, including Coptic work.
The Victoria and Albert Museum, London. Excellent facilities to study the permanent collection. A vast reserve collection, but a long waiting list for scholars wishing to study it.
The Lady Lever Art Gallery, Port Sunlight, Merseyside. A small permanent collection on display.
The Stranger's Hall Museum, Norwich. Some choice samplers displayed in historical context. A good reserve collection, especially rich in plain sewing samplers. May be seen by appointment.
The Castlegate Museum, Nottingham. A small but interesting display, from the seventeenth century to mid-Victorian.
Gawthorpe Hall, Padiham, Near Preston. A comprehensive collection, to be viewed by appointment.
The Bodleian Library, Oxford. A small collection of varied samplers, originals and facsimiles of seventeenth century pattern books, and a collection of Victorian pattern books. Available to senior members of the University and bona fide students who can obtain an introduction to the library.

MATERIALS

Shopping by post

The best way to obtain good materials is to deal with a specialist shop, so obtain and study the catalogue. The main difficulty lies in knowing what to buy, especially as regards coloured threads. Shade cards are obtainable but expensive. There are two alternatives, either to choose your own from threads which have already been pre-selected for you by a buyer who may not have a good colour sense, or to ask a specialist to choose some colour ranges for you. In this way you can soon build up a stock from which to do your own selection.

The Danish Embroidery Centre Ltd, The Old Rectory, Claydon. Ipswich, Suffolk. Selection as at The Danish House, Sloane Street, London.

Mary Allen, Wirksworth, Derbyshire. A very good selection of evenweave fabrics and a wide range of DMC threads, Coton Perlé, Coton à broder.

Mace and Nairn, 89 Crane Street, Salisbury, Wiltshire. An excellent selection of materials and threads, including Danish Flower Thread and Danish Mat Garn. These threads are ideal for counted thread work, and have a beautiful range of colours.

Personal shoppers, even in London, may be disappointed not to find all that they require in one shop. Do not forget to look for coarse evenweave fabrics in furnishing fabric departments in big stores.

Needles

These are generally available.
Milward's Tapestry Nos. 18, 20, 22, 24. Milward's Crewel Nos. 1–10. The higher the number, the finer the needle.

Threads and fabrics

The Royal School of Needlework, 25 Princes Gate, Kensington, London SW7 1QE. A good range of evenweave fabrics, and Clark's Anchor range of threads.

The Danish House, 16 Sloane Street, London SW1. Evenweave cotton fabrics and Danish Flower Threads.

METRICATION

Whilst metrication in the United Kingdom is well advanced, it has not yet extended to fabrics for embroidery, which are still quoted and sold in threads to the inch (or threads to 2.5 cm).

To avoid unnecessary complication, the inch is used as the basic unit of measurement throughout this book, and accordingly the graph paper is divided into 10 small squares to the inch (which is the size most generally available. In case of difficulty, a brief conversion table may be useful.

1 inch = 2.5 cm
1 foot = 0.304 m
1 yard = 0.914 m
1 sq inch = 6.45 sq cm
1 sq foot = 92.90 sq cm
1 sq yard = 0.836 sq m

BIBLIOGRAPHY

D. King, *Samplers*, H.M.S.O.

A. Colby, *Samplers, Yesterday and Today*, Batsford.

A. F. Kendrick, *English Needlework*, A. and C. Black.

P. Wardle, *Guide to English Embroidery*, H.M.S.O.

M. Swain, *Historical Needlework. A study of influences in Scotland and the North of England*, Barrie and Jenkins.

A. G. I. Christie, *Samplers and Stitches*, Batsford.

Elizabeth Geddes and Moyra McNeil, *Blackwork Embroidery*, Dover.

N. V. Wade, *The Basic Stitches of Embroidery*, H.M.S.O.

E. S. Bolton and E. J. Coe, *American Samplers*, Dover.

DESIGN SOURCES

Sampler 1. The Owl on the Vine. Design taken from V & A T190–1960. (The Hind and the Daisies is another set of patterns taken from the same source.)

Sampler 2. The Three Pears. Designs taken from V & A T262–1927 and T99–1925.

Sampler 3. Acorns, Carnations and Pomegranates. Designs taken from V & A T222–1926, 516 and A1877, and T194–1927.

Sampler 4. Blackwork. Designs taken from V & A 516 and A1877, and Fitzwilliam, Cambridge, 1928–129.

Sampler 5. Acorns and Strawberries. Designs taken from V & A T222–1926, T82–1913, T112–1929 and T194–1927, C44–1908.

Sampler 6. White Work. Designs taken from V & A 751–1902, 591–1899, 742–1899, 269–1898, 323–1976, T18–1948, and Fitzwilliam, Cambridge, 7–1938.

Sampler 7. Alphabets. Designs taken from V & A T48–1925, T54–1934.

Sampler 8. Spring. Designs taken from samplers in the National Museum of Wales (St Fagan's).

Sampler 9. Darning. The designs are common to most darning samplers, so no specific design sources are quoted.

Sampler 10. Home and Abroad. Designs taken from Fitzwilliam 40–21, National Museum of Wales 20–254–44, The Bodleian and Embroiderers' Guild Collections, and from a sampler in the author's possession.

Acknowledgements

The author wishes to acknowledge the help of the following: Miss Levy of the Victoria and Albert Museum, Dr. Anthony of the National Museum of Wales, Mrs. Humphrey of the Fitzwilliam Museum, Cambridge, Mrs. Cunningham of Guildford Museum and Miss D. Smith of The Norwich Museum. She is also grateful for the help of Mrs. M. Quick and Mrs. E. Wickham. Thanks are due to all the museums listed under Design Sources, and to the Embroiderers' Guild, for permission to draw from samplers in their collections

and to reproduce the following copyright photographs:
The Fitzwilliam Museum, Cambridge: T1–1928, p36, T11–1952, p80.
The London Museum: p36, and the Victoria and Albert Museum:
T234–1928, p10, T190–1960, p15, 480–1894, p36, T296–1916, p73,
T33A–1935, p75, T36-1945, p94, T250–1920, p103.

Museum references to drawings in the text
The Bodleian Library: *A Schole-house for the Needle*, p32, 33.
The Needle's Excellency, p33. *Works of Learned Ladies*, p38, 40, 55, 111.
J. Johnson Collection, p112.
The Embroiderer's Guild: 1486, p82. 1629, p99. 27, p99.
The Fitzwilliam Museum, Cambridge: 152–1928, p5, 76. 57–1928,
p8, 9, 40. 7–1938, p46, 68. 135–28, p79.
The Guildford Museum: 9.638, p7.
The National Museum of Wales: *passim* p77, 81, 82.
The Victoria and Albert Museum: T194–1927, p6, 42, 55. 288–1886,
p7. 973, p9, 45. 516–A1877, p11, 53. T262–1927, 25, 29. T99–1925,
p29. T222–1926, p35, 42, 48. 829–1902, p37. T82–1913, p37.
T112–1929, p37, 58. 11–1909, p40. T190–1960, p53. 751–1902,
p59. 205–1923, p70. T22–1944, p76. T48–1925, p79. T116–1931,
p96. T250–1920, p110. T102–1939, p110.

INDEX